PRAISE FOR

If you only read one management book in the near future, let this be it.
Professional Manager magazine

Very convincing. Her book adds weight to the argument for a different approach to leadership development based on embodied experience.
HR Director magazine

No one can deny the uncertainty we each face daily. Jude's insights, drawn from both business settings and working with horses, replace a fear of uncertainty with a sense of hope and opportunity. Her stories inspire, her insights inform and her tips encourage change. Through her work with horses, Jude has developed an intensely human capability: to help leaders recognize their style and improve its impact on others.
Dave Ulrich
Rensis Likert Professor, Ross School of Business, University of Michigan
Partner, the RBL Group

Jude Jennison's leadership lessons show great empathy and creativity. Her ideas are fresh – and they work.
Julia Hobsbawm OBE
Author of Fully Connected: Social Health in an Age of Overload *and Honorary Visiting Professor in Workplace Social Health, Cass Business School, London*

A thoroughly engaging, human and insightful book and definitely one for now!
Gina Lodge
CEO, Academy of Executive Coaching

Leaders transform complexity to clarity and uncertainty to understanding. Get Jude's new book to move into deeper clarity and deeper understanding in order to navigate change with grace, authenticity, connection and presence.

Kevin Cashman
Global Head of CEO and Executive Development, Korn Ferry
Best-selling author of Leadership from the Inside Out
and The Pause Principle

An uncertain landscape has become the one certainty for business and good leadership has become even more important. This book is for all those who want to ensure they can lead their organizations through these challenging times. Practical insight from those who've 'been there, done that' and some very different approaches to the challenges of leadership.

Ian O'Donnell MBE
Director, FSB and Head of Policy for the West
Midlands Combined Authority

Wholehearted, engaging and compassionate. Jude Jennison's second book delivers powerful truths and insights into successful leadership in the face of uncertainty. This book positions business struggles as human struggles, allowing leaders to embrace the unknown in an embodied and authentic way in order to move through to what's next.

Dr Veronica Lac PhD
Founder of the HERD Institute and author of the book
Equine-Facilitated Psychotherapy and Learning:
The Human-Equine Relational Development (HERD) Approach

This book is a key narrative at a time when change and the implication of change has never created more pressure on leaders and leadership.

Martin Yardley
Deputy Chief Executive (Place), Coventry City Council

Humans can think, they can emotionalize, they can make good decisions, they can make bad decisions, they can be creative and innovative, they can be mean and fight each other. In short, they are what they are supposed to be and do. If they 'find' the link back to their natural roots, where they belong, they have a better chance of understanding themselves and moving forward. Jude Jennison gives us these ideas through her book. By reading it, your mind will definitely be challenged!!!

Professor Alexandros Psychogios
Professor in International Human Resources Management,
Birmingham City Business School

Jude Jennison understands the complexity of modern-day leadership and the pressure leaders of today are under to perform at their very best. Jude's approach, through working with her horses, places a spotlight on your skills and ability to adapt in unfamiliar surroundings. The results are powerful and empowering. A must for anyone who is serious about being the best leader they can be.

Sue Grindrod
Chief Executive, Gower Street Estates Limited t/a
Albert Dock Liverpool

I was struck by Jude's knowledge and insights on leading through uncertainty. Her warm and engaging style brings out the best of the CEOs she has interviewed to make this a valuable book.

Sue Noyes
Non-executive Director and Former CEO,
East Midlands Ambulance Service

If you struggle with your emotions in business, if you don't dare to express your feelings, if you are suppressed by what is around you – take your time and read this book! You will probably find yourself. Definitely you will get a new perspective on leadership.

Gerhard Krebs
Founder of HorseDream and the European Association
of Horse Assisted Education

LEADING THROUGH UNCERTAINTY

MAKING DISRUPTIVE CHANGE WORK FOR HUMANS

2ND EDITION

JUDE JENNISON

First published in Great Britain by Practical Inspiration Publishing, 2018

This edition published 2022

ISBN   9781788603362   (print)
          9781788603386   (epub)
          9781788603379   (mobi)

To my sister Sue
Who provides stability and wisdom for me
in moments of extreme uncertainty

And to my clients
Who step courageously into my field of uncertainty

CONTENTS

FOREWORD

Leading Through Uncertainty, Jude Jennison's second book, provided a powerful narrative and account of the increasingly fast-paced, ever-changing environment of leadership. It guides and challenges us to adapt our behaviour as leaders and to learn new skills – essential if organizations are to thrive and have an engaged, fulfilled and productive workforce in the future.

When it was first published in 2018, uncertainty was, and will always have to be, expected and faced by leaders, and learning how to act and respond will always be a skill they have or will need to develop fast. The Pandemic arrived at the beginning of 2020, with no time for reflection and detailed planning. It needed a "What needs to be done now? and What's next?" strategy.

The first edition of *Leading Through Uncertainty* provided core thought leadership on how to awaken the importance of this key skill for leaders, although now, it seems to have been a distinctly prophetic sign of what was to come.

This second edition is now essential reading for leaders. We have witnessed how some are able to adapt and pivot, actively guiding their people and organizations through the many challenges COVID-19 has brought, and many have thrived. Sadly, we have also seen those who have suffered and not prospered. The stakes for organizations and people are high in navigating uncertainty.

This second edition guides us in the elements we need as leaders to make our teams feel safe and able to be productive, and to create structure and certainty out of chaos and confusion, laying open the need for leaders to be resilient, have vision, be decisive, adaptable and at the same time, understanding, caring and compassionate.

This book also focusses on the emotional impact on people and explores the impact of COVID-19 on the restricted contact and mental health issues surfacing now. Leaders need their teams to build the future, and they must also acknowledge the impact that the separation and lack of human connection is starting to have.

And what of the future? This second edition goes beyond acknowledging the arrival of the Pandemic in the world; it also recognizes the qualities that leaders are already using to survey the future direction and how they can predict what is on the horizon and how it could impact their organization. Huge opportunities from tech development such as AI, machine learning and gamification as well as the ongoing video communications are opening up markets, driving accessibility, impacting pricing models, scaling, delivery alternatives and more. Leaders who are thriving are looking to the future and trying to prepare for the next disrupter, which will create further uncertainty, bringing People and Planet as key business stakeholders as a key example.

In *Leading Through Uncertainty* Jude states that "it takes an exceptionally skilled leader to balance the energy of driving results with the softness of nurturing in complete harmony" and in this the gauntlet of challenge is cast. This is our call to action in all organizations.

When running highly respected horse-assisted leadership, team development programmes and coaching through her company Leaders by Nature, Jude is assisted by her team of horses: Kalle, Tiffin, Mr Blue and Admiral, and previously Opus and Gio who both died in 2019. I am sure you will feel connected to these wonderful animals by the end of the book and will learn how they can help develop the vital leadership skill of self-awareness.

Working with horses can indeed put many out of their comfort zone and lead us to see that as soon as we, as leaders, revert to control, we have ceased to trust ourselves and our teams. We are guided in considering how leaders can have a degree of certainty in an uncertain world and how the solid backbone of values that we fall back on in times of uncertainty is key to keeping on track. We learn how to not slip back to old, potentially destructive styles of leaderships in times of uncertainty.

My own experience with horse-facilitated leadership was profound and memorable. Whether we feel fear or vulnerability, it is essential that, for the sake of our organizations, teams and personal wellbeing, we find a path towards calm and effective leadership and face the challenges ahead together.

As Jude Jennison says: We are human after all!

Gina Lodge, CEO, Academy of Executive Coaching (AoEC)

INTRODUCTION

'What do you say and do in those moments of uncertainty? You lead. That's all you can do.'

My inspiration for the first edition of this book came when I was sitting in a field with my dog for four days in July 2016. I was exhausted and in a head spin with a high volume of work and continuously operating out of my comfort zone. I was clear where I was heading but unsure about how to get there. I knew that what I was experiencing was common for many of my clients as the world felt more uncertain on a global scale.

I took myself off for four days, sleeping in a safari tent on a farm with only my black Labrador, Pepsi, for company. We had the most amazing time together, hardly seeing or speaking to anyone, and the result was the title of this book.

A title may not be much output for four days' reflection, but it created a spark, and sometimes we need space for the creativity to come. I returned to work inspired, knowing that the uncertainty experienced in the world was a replica of the uncertainty that my clients and I were also experiencing.

The first edition of this book was duly written and published in May 2018, long before the words 'COVID-19 pandemic' were uttered. Since then, we've experienced a masterclass in uncertainty and disruptive change. We've lived and breathed the content of this book unwittingly, sometimes handling the change with skill and care, sometimes dragging ourselves kicking and screaming through it. I was fascinated to watch everything I'd written about in the first edition play out on a global and magnified scale.

This revised edition includes the latest thinking and research based on the global uncertainty of the COVID-19 pandemic and what that means for business as we navigate the future. I've chosen to avoid talking about politics and what we think about how politicians in different countries handled the pandemic. That debate continues in our everyday society and adds no value to this book, which is intended to reflect on how uncertainty and disruptive change impact leaders in business. However, you may want to reflect separately on how politicians are also impacted by everything I write about in this book. More honesty about the impact of disruptive change on them personally might support greater transparency in government and the media.

When the first edition of this book was published, there was recognition of the uncertainty but a desire by most people to still seek to be in control. In the aftermath of COVID-19, there is a greater understanding of the impact of extreme and long-lasting uncertainty. We've both witnessed and experienced the impact of disruptive change. We've demonstrated inordinate resilience in the face of adversity, and businesses have demonstrated their ability to rapidly pivot to survive – and in some cases thrive. Those who have not, or who were in sectors that could not, have closed. Such is the impact of disruptive change, and it's here to stay.

In addition, much to many people's surprise, the emotional fallout of disruptive change that this book initially sought to highlight came to the fore. There were great examples of leaders engaging their teams, with a heightened understanding of the need to manage mental health in order to get the best from their employees.

As life and work become more stable, and as we learn to live with the pandemic, the emotional impact of the disruptive change lives on. A traumatic event takes its emotional toll in the longer term, and ongoing disruptive change in business has a similar impact. We can't just 'crack on' with a Blitz spirit. It's not sustainable or reasonable in the complex world we inhabit today.

The twenty-first century was already one of disruptive change and uncertainty. The COVID-19 pandemic has accelerated the pace and disruption yet further. The next 10 years are likely to transform beyond recognition as new technology continues to disrupt the way we live and work.

Throughout the book, I touch on the key challenges facing leaders in disruptive change. I explore the need to evolve quickly and adapt to uncertainty, and I highlight the skills needed to make disruptive change work for humans.

How we lead in business and the decisions we take fundamentally shape the world and society. The responsibility of leadership lies with each and every one of us.

The challenge of uncertainty

Uncertainty is uncomfortable. It is something to be embraced rather than feared, but it requires a shift in our thinking and behaviour. Uncertainty creates unforeseen opportunities if we are willing to step over the edge and out of our comfort zone. It also creates stress and overwhelm, fear and polarization, and in those moments you may wonder whether you can continue like this. The volume of workload is overwhelming, and the fundamental desire to get everything right and be in control is not possible or sustainable.

Thanks to the pandemic, we all now have an understanding of the discomfort of leading through uncertainty. Leaders need to continue to ease the mental and emotional load, for themselves as well as for their team. Uncertainty generates a wealth of emotions that we must face head on and accept as being part of the process. We can minimize those emotions by adapting our behaviour and developing new skills.

In addition to the pressures of work, we are human beings experiencing the challenges of life. As work and life are more integrated than ever before, the challenges we face become more difficult to balance.

Life is not certain for any of us. We can plan for things as much as possible, but events will always happen outside of our control. We can choose how we respond, and our choices have consequences.

Uncertainty has a cycle. It requires a letting go of one thing so something new can emerge. When we entered the first lockdown of the COVID-19 pandemic, we let go of perfection and being physically face to face in order to shift to remote working overnight. It was an unexpected social experiment to create technological and behavioural change in 24 hours on a global scale. Many organizations prided themselves on their rapid response to logistical and technological issues. The emotional impact was wider, more complex and ongoing.

We are all somewhat unskilled in uncertainty, but we are all also skilled in it. We have moments when we have no idea what to do and moments when we are willing to risk everything and take a stand for what we believe in.

We spend huge amounts of time imparting knowledge, believing we need to have the answers.

> *Uncertainty provides an opportunity to step into "How can we…?" and "What is needed now?" This is a paradigm shift from knowing to not knowing, from individual knowledge and power to collective wisdom and collaboration.*

Throughout this book, I explore how leaders in organizations must recognize the human challenges that we face in uncertainty and embrace them in leadership. Disruptive change is here to stay. Our role as leaders is to meet the associated challenges with curiosity, compassion, gentleness, and courage, and make disruptive change work for humans and society as well as for business and economics.

Horses and uncertainty

In the course of my work as an executive coach and strategic leadership partner, I bring clients to work with my herd of horses. It may sound strange but the horses invite clients to return to their true nature while working in an environment of uncertainty and unpredictability. It provides an opportunity for people to explore how they lead out of their comfort zone. Working with horses creates an embodied experience of leadership where people flex their leadership style, find new ways of leading and increase self-awareness through feedback.

My clients work with me and the horses on the ground. No riding is involved. Once you put a rider on a horse's back, the relationship changes. When you work with a horse on the ground, it is based on pure partnership where neither party has ultimate control over what happens. It provides an environment for people to explore a different way of leading that is more relational, more collaborative, and based on engaging and inspiring others to work with you.

Horses are masters of sensing beyond the words, and they provide non-judgemental feedback on your non-verbal communication. They don't care who you are or what job you do. They want to know whether you can lead them to safety, be clear about where you are going and include them in the decision-making through a solid relationship based on trust, mutual respect, confidence, and compassion. The hierarchy is definitely flat when you enter the paddock. Your negotiation skills are about to be put to their greatest test. By including horses in the exploration, people show up more fully and gain greater insights into where their leadership is in flow and where it is not, thus allowing an opportunity for recalibration throughout the day.

Research shows that in the presence of horses, you align the head, heart and gut, combining the wisdom of your intellect with your emotions and gut instinct. The human race has been trained to rely on the information in our brains, yet we have so much more wisdom in our reach. When we align the intellect with our emotions and gut instincts, we are more authentic, have more clarity and behave in a more congruent manner.

A client leading Kalle

By their very nature, horses appear to be unpredictable to most people. That's largely because we don't always understand their behaviour. As a prey animal, their primary goal is the safety of the herd. They work as a cohesive unit and share responsibility for their collective safety.

Working with horses provides an environment of uncertainty where your leadership is in the spotlight. The horses require the same qualities of a leader that a human team requires – clarity, direction, and purpose, balanced with relationships based on trust and mutual respect. They need all of this to feel safe, as people do too. Ultimately, the horses want to know that you are authentic and acting with integrity. If you create an environment that makes them feel safe, they come with you; if you don't, they plant their feet and refuse to move. Either way is feedback and a chance to recalibrate and expand your leadership capabilities by trying new approaches.

When people first meet the horses, they are often scared because they don't know whether the horses will cooperate. The uncertainty is obvious. The sheer size and presence of horses can be intimidating and invoke anxiety. Some people say they've never met anyone bigger and stronger than them, and it immediately poses a threat. This is especially true for men, many of whom often unconsciously use their physicality to exert power, whereas women are used to not being physically the strongest in the room.

> *Overpowering a horse physically is not the answer. Telling them what to do because you are the boss doesn't work here. Being a people pleaser won't get you a result either. The horses want to know that you can lead them through uncertainty, balancing clarity and focused action with strong relationship skills.*

I often start the day by explaining that I don't know what is going to happen. The day is full of uncertainty and the unknown – and not just for the clients. I watch people shrink back at that moment. There is an expectation that as the leader of the day, at my venue with my horses, I should be 'in charge' and 'in control'. That's a myth. I lead through uncertainty with every client. I never know how people will show up and how the horses will respond. I'm constantly flexing my approach. It's a relational exchange that requires great skill and care. Many of the skills involved are included in this book.

The best we can hope for in any given moment is to lead and to make decisions based on the information we have available – not just intellectual information, facts, and logic, but also the information that we gain from our emotions and our gut instinct. Both of these provide us with great insights into what action we might want to take as a leadership choice in any given moment. Emotions and gut instinct have largely been dismissed in favour of logic and reasoning, but they are increasingly critical to the success of business.

Where are you striving to be 'in control'?

What happens when you loosen your grip?

Your emotions offer an important source of information. If you are terrified when you first come face to face with a horse, it is feedback that you can use as a guide to how you might approach them and the first leading exercise. It would be foolish to put yourself into a situation that causes you to instantly reach a place of overwhelm, yet many find themselves in this situation in the workplace. In a moment of sheer terror, the wise option might be to ask for help, to reflect and observe or to seek more information to help guide your decision. How many people do that at work?

Alternatively, if you feel relaxed when you first come face to face with a horse, then the next step of leading one is not as big and might take you only slightly out of your comfort zone. Part of what people learn is how to challenge themselves out of the comfort zone and how to create safety and support in doing so.

Everyone's comfort zone is different, based on values, beliefs, experience, self-awareness and self-esteem, and much more. There is no right or wrong baseline, but it is interesting to know where your benchmark is.

How comfortable are you leading through uncertainty?

People's default patterns of behaviour show up around the horses. Some of my clients are confident with the unknown and are able to lead effectively, even if they feel anxious. Others are terrified to the point of overwhelm and need more support to achieve the same task.

One client explained that she had stayed in her comfort zone and never spoke up in meetings, believing being out of her comfort zone to be 'dangerous'. After working with me and my horses, she realized she was uncomfortable but that was not the same as dangerous. Her organization was leading substantial and disruptive change that she had been anxious about. After working with the horses, she felt more confident stepping out of her comfort zone, no longer feeling unsafe. As a result, she embraced the change with confidence and spoke up more in meetings, adding more value.

> *Horses respond based on non-verbal feedback and provide a great opportunity to experience where you get out of your comfort zone and how you recover to a place of confident leadership in uncertainty.*

Background to this book

My leadership career began at IBM, where I worked for 17 years. I held a variety of roles in the outsourcing business, and in the latter years of my career I regularly led disruptive change, often at a European or global level. I learned to provide clarity of direction and engage a team to work with me in some challenging senior leadership roles – always leading through uncertainty. I did jobs that were undefined, creating structure and certainty out of chaos and confusion. However, it was only in 2011, when I overcame my fear of horses and started working with them, that I really understood what it took to be an effective leader in uncertainty.

This book is born out of my combined leadership experience of working in the corporate world, running a small business and especially working with horses. I draw on both my experience and my clients' experiences of working with horses to highlight the key concepts of leading through uncertainty, as well as including interviews with leaders from all walks of life. Of course, our experience of the COVID-19 pandemic was a masterclass in disruptive change and how to lead through uncertainty too.

Every day I lead through uncertainty.

Each time I lead a horse, I don't know whether my leadership is enough.

Will the horse come with me? Will I be safe? Am I clear enough? Is the relationship strong enough? Can I achieve what I want to achieve?

Although I don't dwell on these questions, they are always there in uncertainty. With little horse experience, I have only my leadership to fall back on. The horses will not go along with anyone or anything they don't want to. Neither will people. They may come grudgingly or unwillingly for a time, but leaders need to energize employees and organizations better at times of disruptive change. When I took ownership of my first horse in December 2011 and started delivering Equine Facilitated Leadership, I recognized that leaders were operating against a backdrop of uncertainty in their work. I was living and breathing it daily every time I led a horse, as leaders were in their everyday work, sometimes realizing it, more often not. When I talked about uncertainty with clients, I observed the discomfort they had with that word. Their desire to achieve results meant they were reluctant to admit that they might not be in control. Yet we are never in control.

Over time, the word 'uncertainty' became normalized. Brexit in the United Kingdom created the first period of uncertainty, and people began to recognize that the world was not as certain as they had previously thought. We could no longer pretend that we were in control. The COVID-19 pandemic has exacerbated this further. Every country has responded to the pandemic in a slightly different way. Time will tell who has handled it the best; it's only in hindsight that we can really be sure. In the midst of disruptive change, the outcomes of the decisions we make continue to be uncertain, even though we may believe they are certain.

One common response to uncertainty is an increase in fear and polarization as we have to make decisions without all the data. Fear and polarization are now endemic, the topic of mental health has risen further on the agenda of organizations, and there is a recognition that uncertainty is here to stay. Despite our deep-rooted desire for security and certainty, COVID-19 brought the term 'uncertainty' further to the fore, teaching us levels of resilience never before experienced in peacetime.

Stress arises when we try to force specific outcomes that are out of our control. I've repeatedly watched clients try to exert control, only to discover that they get better results by softening their approach, letting go of attachment to a particular way and relaxing into their leadership. I witness them develop greater flexibility, adaptability, and collaboration, leading to faster results. I believe our leadership is at its best when we allow it to be easy. That in itself is a challenge!

How this book is structured

This book is intended to provide insights to the challenges we face of leading through uncertainty and the skills needed to lead disruptive change. It encourages you to understand the emotional challenges that uncertainty invokes, and to explore how you can overcome them by recognizing that we are human.

In Part 1, I explore the context within which we are working today. I explain why I work with horses, how I came to work with them, the radical change we are experiencing in the world of work, the challenges we face as a human species in a technological world of disruptive change, the need to evolve our leadership and why compelling use of emotions is crucial for effective leadership.

Part 2 explores the underlying emotional challenges we face when leading through uncertainty. I explain how uncertainty causes stress and overwhelm, and how fear and polarization are a fundamental part of navigating uncertainty. I explore how past experiences, pain and trauma influence our default habits and behaviours. We cannot expect to resolve and eradicate emotional responses; instead, we must include them in our leadership.

Jude leading Opus (left) and Mr Blue (right)

Parts 3 to 5 provide the leadership skills we need to develop to lead confidently through disruptive change and support our teams and organizations. Part 3 sets out why we need to lead by example. It examines the importance of creating clarity in the chaos of disruptive change and how to lead confidently and competently through disruption, even if you don't have all the answers.

Part 4 covers the humanity of change, exploring how you lead others through uncertainty to minimize the stress, overwhelm, fear, and polarization. These are essential skills in uncertainty and they are critical to our ability to be more compassionate in the workplace. Resilience has its limits, and we can't match computers for speed and processing power. We must find ways to look after ourselves and each other so we can collaborate and find inclusive solutions together.

Part 5 explores the need for self-care and compassion at a time of emotional turmoil. Many leaders in the COVID-19 pandemic were so focused on supporting others that they nearly burned themselves out in the process. Self-care in disruptive change is a critical part of the process of leadership.

Each chapter opens with an illustrative horse story, key concepts are highlighted in boxed statements and thought-provoking questions are accentuated in italics. Each chapter ends with pointers to master uncertainty, followed by questions aimed at provoking personal insight and self-reflection. Throughout the book, there are case studies from business leaders which provide examples of where more than one client has had the same or a similar experience. Names have been changed to protect client confidentiality. In some chapters, there are contributions from other industry leaders where appropriate.

Throughout the book, I make reference to client experiences with the horses and what they learn, but mostly this is a book about uncertainty and leadership. For more information on how I work with horses, my first book, *Leadership Beyond Measure*, provides substantial background, theory, and case studies, as well as my own learning from horses. While the client case studies are true examples of what can happen, they reflect the experience of many people rather than one individual.

 Where you see this symbol, you will find reference to additional content, which is downloadable from my website at www.judejennison.com/uncertainty. This includes a workbook to capture your personal insights, white papers, and other resources.

This book explains that however much you plan for every eventuality, nothing is certain in life, and we can lead in a new way without being reactive.

Part 1
THE CONTEXT OF UNCERTAINTY

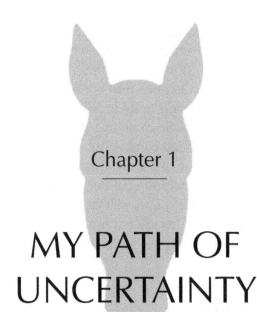

Chapter 1

MY PATH OF UNCERTAINTY

'If you can lead a horse, you can lead anyone.'

'That's a lot of horse!' I thought.

That was an understatement. Kalle was majestic. I watched her gallop up and down the arena. With her mane and tail flying behind her and her head held high, she snorted loudly as she charged from one end to the other. It was clear that she was strong, powerful, and opinionated. I knew nothing about horses, but she certainly didn't look like a horse who was suitable for a novice such as me.

I had no reference point for this moment. I had only recently overcome my fear of horses. My previous experiences had included six months riding at the age of nine and three serious accidents around horses as an adult, one while I was riding and two others on the ground. I write about these more extensively in *Leadership Beyond Measure* so I won't go into them here. What I will say is that I was a novice, and I knew very little about horses. The only thing that was certain was that I was here to look at a horse to work with me. Despite Kalle charging up and down at an alarming rate, I walked calmly into the arena and stood in the middle. Having overcome my fear of horses only six months earlier, it seemed a brave thing to do. I'm not sure why I did it, but I followed my instincts and stepped into the arena of uncertainty. I felt as though my heart would stop, and I breathed deeply.

As soon as I walked in, Kalle came to a stop at the other end of the arena. I stayed calm, breathing consciously and grounding myself. She walked over to me and stood by my right shoulder. She looked me deep in the eyes, and I felt the soul-to-soul connection that she creates so magically. I gulped and felt my eyes well up with tears. I was moved by the power and gentleness of her spirit. I walked forward and Kalle came with me. I stopped and she stopped with me. I paused, trying to breathe.

Kalle gallops at full speed

I moved again, turning left and right, stopping and starting. Kalle matched me step for step. When I moved, she came. When I stopped, she did too. The connection felt so deep yet I had no idea what I was doing. I had virtually no experience around horses. I had stepped right out of my depth and dived head-first into the deep end of uncertainty.

I was completely unskilled in looking after a horse. I was uncertain whether she was suitable or whether I could handle her. I could feel the power of her palpating beside me, and my heart was pounding. She was choosing to follow me as a leader, even though I had no idea what I was doing. I have received no greater acknowledgement of my leadership than in that moment. Kalle chose to follow with complete free will. It was and continues to be a deeply moving experience.

I went back to the gate to talk to her owner, Julie. Kalle was loose, but she stayed by my side as I went. I said to Julie, 'She's so responsive. She's the kind of horse I could really connect with.' At that moment, Kalle turned, looked me in the eye and nodded. My heart lurched, and I swallowed hard.

I was chosen.

What led me here?

In 2010, I left a 17-year career at IBM. After numerous senior leadership roles, including managing a European budget of US$1 billion, I knew there was more for me in life. In hindsight, I was close to burnout, but I didn't realize it until I took a year's sabbatical and slowed down almost to a stop. After that sabbatical, I set up a leadership and coaching business with the desire to help senior leaders and executives work in harmony by finding their inner peace as well as creating outer peace. I knew what it was like to work in a large organization, feeling ground down under the pressure of a heavy workload with aggressive targets to reach. I knew the stresses and strains of trying to work collaboratively in a high-pressure, high-performance culture with no let-up. I also knew how energizing, exciting, and rewarding it could be. The uncertainty of disruptive change is immense, and we often overlook the need to recharge. Some people thrive on it, others are left reeling.

Having completed a year-long transformational leadership programme with The Coaches Training Institute, I also knew there was another way to lead, if only people had the skills to do so. Ironically, in the times when we are under pressure to succeed, there is a tendency to speed up, and in so doing we often lose our ability to lead effectively. What is needed in those moments is a slower, more grounded pace, a way of connecting to your authentic leadership and finding your flow with ease. Athletes know what it is like to be in the zone and spend years working with a performance coach to help them achieve it. Leaders who find this flow are not only powerful, compelling, and engaging, they are often less stressed, more grounded and calmer. It makes good business sense to create an environment for leaders to thrive in this way. Yet in the current world of fast-paced change, everything is uncertain, and few people find the space to create that flow.

Following my heart

When I left my corporate career, everyone said I was courageous, and some wished they could leave too. Why didn't they? Fear of uncertainty and fear of failure. Although I had substantial experience working in a large global corporation of more than 400,000 employees worldwide, and I was comfortable managing a European budget of US$1 billion, nothing could have prepared me for running a small business on my own. When I added horses into the mix, the uncertainty grew exponentially. Everything was unknown. I was on my own with no support structure, and the learning curve was fast. Failure was a definite possibility.

Over the coming months and years, I would fail repeatedly, pick myself up and try again. Disruptive change is uncomfortable because we have a psychological need for safety. Uncertainty is a threat to our safety, yet it is unavoidable if we want to create breakthroughs.

One of the first leadership programmes I ran was a six-month programme for a group of IT directors. It was called 'Challenge the Status Quo' and was designed to help them increase self-awareness and be more bold and courageous in their leadership. In between workshops, I gave them practical challenges to develop their leadership further, one of which was to overcome their fear of something. I'm a great believer in walking my talk and won't ask anyone to do anything I wouldn't be willing to do myself. And so I found myself working with someone to help me overcome my fear of horses. Despite my fear, I kept being drawn to horses without knowing why. I had no intention of riding again, so my decision to overcome my fear of them was to put the fear to rest and move on.

Little did I know what was in store. I overcame my fear of horses in the first five minutes of being in their presence and learned so much about my own leadership in the first two hours. I talk about this experience in more detail in *Leadership Beyond Measure*. Suffice to say here that I discovered Equine Facilitated Leadership, which is a way of working with horses to develop leadership and communication skills.

Following that first session, instead of putting my fascination with horses to rest, it was reignited, and I found myself drawn to learning more about working with them. Still with no intention of doing the work, I embarked on an extensive training programme to work specifically with corporate leaders and teams.

Uncertainty was at play in abundance.

Throughout the training, I found myself working with people who had their own horses and were very confident and competent around them. I was unsure why I was doing the training, but I followed my instincts and trusted that I was meant to be there. I was willing to explore and see what happened. The only thing that was certain was that it felt right. In moments of uncertainty, we tend to rely on logic and reasoning, yet our instincts are rarely wrong. Effective leaders trust their intuition in uncertainty and include it in the decision-making process.

I had no desire to ride horses, yet there was also no doubt that I was in the right place. In only eight months, I overcame my fear, qualified as a HorseDream Partner, delivered my first corporate workshop and took ownership of my first horse.

Life was moving fast, and I was galloping along the path of uncertainty with no idea where I was heading.

Facing uncertainty head on

After seeing Kalle charging up and down the arena, I knew deep down that she was the right horse for me. My heart was sure, my gut instinct was clear, but my head was questioning the sanity of taking on such a majestic animal when my capabilities of handling horses were virtually non-existent. I didn't even know how to put on a head collar.

I went home to think about it. I wanted to be sure I was doing the right thing. In moments of uncertainty, we look for certainty – glimpses that we are on the right track. Things were moving fast, and I felt the need to slow down the decision and give myself time to pause for breath. Kalle is 16.2 hands high (which is 1.68 metres to the top of the shoulder), bigger than I had intended as a first horse. She is a German breed called Trakehner, known for being spirited and highly sensitive. Riders often say this breed is tricky to handle. Knowing nothing about horses, I was oblivious to this. I discovered that they are highly sensitive and intuitive, making them perfect for my work.

I had limited experience around horses, and this was a huge decision. At the time, many people said I was bold. Others told me I was crazy. I didn't see it in either of those ways. When people questioned my capability, I replied that nobody knows how to look after a child until they have one – you just have to learn. And fast! I followed my heart and knew that this was the work I wanted to do. Exactly eight months after I overcame my fear of horses, Kalle came into my life. Clients had been asking to work with horses, so I decided I'd better get a horse!

If I had any doubts about taking on a horse as powerful as Kalle, I was certain my friends would not let me play small. Later that day, I spoke to a dear friend, Nicole, and explained that Kalle was big, powerful, spirited, kind, and gentle, and that I was a little concerned that she might be too much for clients. Nicole asked whether I could handle her. I replied that I thought so. To which Nicole responded, 'If you think you can handle her and your clients can't, then you are holding your clients too small.' With that I made the decision. I took ownership of Kalle one month later.

My path of uncertainty had most definitely begun.

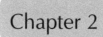

Chapter 2

TECHNOLOGY AND DISRUPTIVE CHANGE

'When you reach your limit, stop, reflect and find another way. The challenge is to know when your limit has been reached.'

'Sit down and be quiet.'

The words of my childhood years at school. I was told what to do and how to do it, and I was expected to follow the instructions. I was rewarded when I did and reprimanded when I fell short. Things were fairly black and white. Pretty certain. The world looks very different today.

Now you are competing against technology for your job. You're not a robot, but you may sometimes feel like one.

Many people do the workload of three people but are not considered resilient enough when they get stressed.

Change is constant and disruptive, but resistance or questioning is frowned upon. You're expected to 'be on the bus'.

You are technologically connected, causing an 'always on' mentality, often leading to an increase in stress levels.

We've adapted technologically to remote and hybrid working but it takes more effort and energy – effort and energy we lack in the aftermath of the pandemic. The emotional impact continues to wreak havoc and raise more questions than we have answers.

You are not superhuman. Something has to give.

Rapid pace of change

Have you ever wished there were more hours in the day? Do you find yourself permanently rushing from one place to another? Do you get to the end of the day only to discover you haven't achieved the things you planned to do?

We live in extraordinary times. Life and work are changing at an alarming pace in ways we cannot predict, and at times it leaves people feeling exposed, uneasy and uncomfortable. People are increasingly connected to technology and disconnected on an emotional and physical level.

Who are you disconnected from?

The rapid advances in technology drive disruptive change in every area of our lives. We need to continually adapt fast, and every change creates uncertainty. Technological advances are ahead of our use of it. For example, many businesses were resistant to remote working, believing it would not be effective. The COVID-19 pandemic showed that we can adapt rapidly to using technology and working in a different way. The technology already existed. We shifted to using it overnight, but what was technically possible had an emotional impact that we must not step over.

The rapid shift to remote working led many people to question how they work. Many have enjoyed being more hands on with their family or having the company of their dog under their desk. Disruptive change always causes us to rethink our priorities. We must recognize that when we implement disruptive change in the workplace, it will have a major impact on the engagement of employees. How do you engage them in the change and make it work for everyone?

As the world adopts a hybrid way of working, everyone has a different opinion about how companies should manage the working environment. This creates further uncertainty and raises many fundamental questions to which we don't yet have answers:

- How do executive teams handle the uncertainty of the future?
- How do employees adapt to disruptive change?
- How do we manage mental health in an ever-increasing pace of change?
- Who is driving disruptive change, or is it being thrust upon us by external events?

When we entered the first lockdown of the COVID-19 pandemic in March 2020, organizations shifted their whole business from the office to remote working. The rapid response and adaptability to achieve that shift in 24 hours is unprecedented and astonishing. Yet the emotional impact must not be overlooked. What is deemed a technological triumph has in many cases been an emotional disaster, with many people left reeling and trying to come to terms with the changes thrust upon them.

We are not machines and we need to emotionally process change in a way that computers do not. What is logistically and technologically possible may not be emotionally viable. The ever-increasing pace of change is not sustainable for human beings. We are bombarded by information, but we cannot process it at the same pace as a computer does. As computer processing power increases in speed, our view of what is possible becomes further skewed, and people put themselves under increased pressure to try to keep up. The uncertainty of operating in an environment like this is immense, and the continuous uncertainty and pressure can lead to overwhelm and overload.

Working in this way can result in burnout and mental health issues. When the pressure is on to deliver, human connection is one of the first things to suffer. We have to find another way to use technology instead of being used by it. We go to great lengths to provide the right environment for technology to work. We need to afford people the environment where they can thrive too, whether that is in the office, working remotely or a combination of the two. Human connection is paramount and an essential need.

Human beings vs supercomputers

Human beings process information in a contextual way, which includes the environment, emotions, and the systems around us. We get distracted by information because we emotionally engage with it, whereas computers do not.

Computers can process high volumes of data, sort it logically and provide output that enables us to make decisions effectively. Computers don't have a finite capacity because we can upgrade them and expand their capacity whereas the human capacity for processing is finite. If your phone fills up with photos, you either delete information or upgrade the phone to hold more. You cannot currently upgrade your brain to process information faster. I hope you never will, although it is highly possible in the future. As human beings, we have expanded our capabilities for decades in parallel to the processing power of computers. We need to recognize that we have our limits when it comes to processing information and that we need to operate within them. We must ensure we retain the core of our humanity and work alongside technology without needing to become it.

If we use computers and robots to do the work that we can't do, we can focus on the core of what makes us human, which is creativity and thought leadership, embracing the skills of nurturing, community, and connection. We can do that without burning out and having a nervous breakdown.

We have trained our brains to operate at high speed and don't know how to switch off. We are more overstimulated than ever before, and our brains are constantly whirring, leading to stress and overwhelm. As technology evolves, we are unconsciously making the assumption that we can evolve at the same pace of processing. All of this exacerbates the uncertainty.

Where are you running at full speed, and where do you need to slow down?

Technology drives the pace of work and change, and we cannot control the quality and volume of information that exists in the world today.

Either we respond to technological advances, or we become obsolete in the marketplace. The COVID-19 pandemic was a great example of that. Many small businesses transformed rapidly to generate new online offerings to stay in business. That was easier in some sectors – for example, retail and professional services. Other sectors that rely on physical face-to-face activity, such as tourism, travel, and hospitality, were severely impacted by the disruption. Many pubs, cafes and restaurants quickly switched to takeaway and delivery services. Many of these were temporary measures. For others, they implemented new digital solutions that can coexist longer term with face-to-face offerings.

Gio and Mr Blue chase each other in the snow

One great example is Innovating Minds, a social enterprise based in Birmingham in the United Kingdom. CEO Dr Asha Patel set up her social enterprise to enable children and families to access early interventions for their mental health. Her business model was previously based on psychologists visiting schools and working within the community to support children. She digitized her enterprise so she could reach schools and front-line practitioners nationally without having to significantly increase overhead costs. This business model has enabled Innovating Minds to scale its social impact and quickly respond to children's mental health needs.

Dr Patel said:

> As a clinician I never imagined myself building tech products and successfully taking them to market in a short space of time. It has come with its challenges, the organization structure has changed and the team had to adapt to a SaaS [software as a service] model. The transformation has been remarkable as we have significantly increased our social impact, and the team are capitalizing on their strengths as leaders to become the leading social enterprise to enable access to early mental health support.

Technology-based businesses disrupt the way we live and work, and that creates uncertainty for legacy businesses that need to adapt quickly to survive. Those that lack the agility to adapt quickly and be flexible could lose their jobs or their businesses. Uncertainty and the rapidly changing world work for those who are early adopters and fast to respond. If you are in this camp, it's easier, but for many of your team, it may be much harder to embrace change. We need to help people adapt to this new way of behaving.

Data and information drive our behaviour. Smartphones, tablets, and nanotechnology tell us what to eat, when to move, how to meditate and so on. We must consider how we use technology and how it drives our decisions, both now and in the future.

The ethics of technology

Technology raises questions of ethics to consider and address. The rise of artificial intelligence (AI) has major implications for the future of work, business, employees, society and the human race. With women continuing to be under-represented in technology-based businesses, AI is largely programmed by a white male demographic. With our increased understanding of unconscious bias, it's reasonable to assume that technology will exacerbate white male privilege. That should raise alarm bells for all of us.

The Deloitte Global Human Capital Trends report 2017 indicates that the pace of change of technology is growing exponentially, followed by people, business and lastly public bodies. Government organizations and public bodies are slow to respond to the impact of technological change. When new technology is released, nobody can be sure what will be widely adopted and how it might influence how we live and work. Our lives are dominated by the power of big technology businesses, such as Amazon and Facebook. If technology businesses determine our future, and if government organizations and public bodies don't provide the guidelines, who will?

The vast changes in business and society create uncertainty for all of us in both our working and personal lives. It is possible to use technology as a force for good, to create opportunities and enhance society, but it relies on the few who make those decisions to consider the impact from all angles. It is the responsibility of every leader to ensure that the decisions we make *are* enhancing and *do* benefit society in the longer term. It's not acceptable for leaders to line their own pockets with bonuses and pay rises without considering the enormous impact we have as leaders, and the responsibility we take for shaping the future of our world.

> *Our decisions create an impact, consciously or unconsciously. It is the responsibility of all business leaders to act wisely and consciously, to create a sustainable future that is life-enhancing for all.*

What decisions are you making today that will affect the future for generations to come?

Artificial intelligence is growing in sophistication, and the current expectation is that 30% of all jobs will be performed by artificial intelligence by 2030. Whether this becomes a reality or not, the role of the employee will continue to change as information and data processing will be performed by computers far faster and more efficiently than humans ever could manage it. This raises some interesting questions about what we value in business and how we reward people.

- How do we reconcile the fact that care workers, nurses, and social workers, whose work cannot be automated, are paid so little compared with lawyers and accountants whose work could be heavily automated in the future?

- How do we redress the balance of pay so that we reward emotional intelligence, social responsibility, compassion, and caring for the community as well as intellect?
- How do we create a world where humanity and inclusivity are as important as information and knowledge, when the latter can be mechanized and the former cannot?

The uncertainty of our time is often driven by external influences. The COVID-19 pandemic was a great example of that. It has led to increased adoption of technology and has wide-reaching implications for all of us. We can use technology to improve the way we live and work if we make decisions consciously, but the ethical debate around technology needs to be considered by all of us.

How can you use technology more consciously and recognize the impact it has on your daily life?

Connection or disconnection?

People use technology as a way of disconnecting from things that feel uncomfortable, such as standing in a queue in a coffee shop, or waiting for a train, bus or taxi. Even in meetings, when things get uncomfortable people distract themselves from the moment by using technology to disconnect from the emotion, as well as from those around them.

> *We use technology to disconnect when the connection or the learning is uncomfortable. It acts as a comfort blanket, something we can rely on to make us feel better in uncomfortable situations.*

As a species, we are more technologically connected and more emotionally disconnected than ever before. Families are widely dispersed globally. As children growing up in the twentieth century, we were in and out of each other's homes, sharing the laughter, the joy, the pain, and the sadness. Emotion was a fundamental part of our lives.

Connection was obvious and effortless, and our sphere of connection and community was local.

In the backdrop of the physical disconnection that remote working brought during the COVID-19 pandemic lockdowns, the desire for connection was evident as a fundamental part of being human. In the absence of face-to-face connection, people seek connection via social media, finding people they agree with, who share their ideas and opinions, shutting down from anyone who may be different. As the world of business seeks to embrace more diverse opinions, the way we use technology creates the opposite approach. Technology influences what you do and don't see, and that impacts your opinions and beliefs, leading to increased polarization and extreme views.

We have an opportunity to use technology to connect rather than disconnect, and we need to be more curious about different opinions in uncertainty. At its worst, technology creates an emotional disconnect that allows polarization and exacerbates online bullying with major consequences. We need the emotional resilience to allow us to be with the differences that world-views bring and the skills to work through those differences.

Collaboration not competition

There is a need to work in collaboration with technology rather than competing with it on pace and output. We are no longer bound by our immediate local community in life and work. Technology can expand your horizons, and that increases the uncertainty. The limitless opportunities for connection and collaboration can be overwhelming, so the tendency can be to shut it down. In addition, the facelessness of technology can lead to disconnection. We cannot see someone's emotional response when we send an email, text or WhatsApp message. While emoticons give you some idea of the sender's emotion, using technology has become a way to avoid the emotional impact of empathy. Instead of giving bad news face to face, people have taken the cowardly way out of communicating via technology. Technology used in this way creates emotional disconnection, which has a major impact on our society.

We need a more conscious awareness of how we use technology going forward to ensure we develop it and use it to enhance business and society.

Technology has had a hugely positive impact on how we live and work, advancing solutions in healthcare, renewable energy, and business in general. It enables us to collaborate globally on projects that we previously could not, expanding the realms of what is possible and embracing different cultures and ways of working.

While research can be performed faster with technology, there is a genuine concern about the quality of the data on the internet. The rise of social media has brought about popular commentary, where anyone can share their opinion as if it were a fact, and much of it is very convincing. We no longer know what to believe and this can cause people to be misguided or, worse, disengaged through overwhelm. Leaders need to focus and gain clarity on what to pay attention to and what to ignore. The ability to sift out important information is critical to how decisions are made.

Successful leaders in the future will integrate technological advances with their innate wisdom and emotions to ensure we increase human connection and make decisions that benefit society and communities in an inclusive way.

How inclusive are your decisions?

Mastering uncertainty

- Notice where technology skews your thinking on what is humanly possible.

- Be aware that you and your team cannot match technology in the speed and volume of data processing.

- Consider the ethics of how you use technology and the impact it has on individuals, business and society.

- Use technology to create connection across borders and cultures.

- Pay attention to where technology creates disconnection, both emotionally and physically.

- Use technology responsibly and ethically to enhance human experience in society.

Before you move on to the next chapter, spend 10 minutes reflecting on how technology affects your behaviour.

Download the *Leading Through Uncertainty* workbook from www.judejennison.com/uncertainty and record your reflections.

Provoking personal insight

Who are you disconnected from?

Where are you running at full speed and do you need to slow down?

What decisions are you making today that will affect the future for generations to come?

How can you use technology more consciously and recognize the impact it has on your daily life?

How inclusive are your decisions?

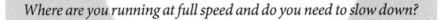

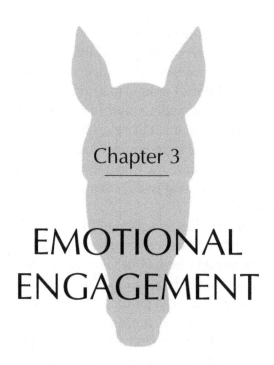

Chapter 3

EMOTIONAL ENGAGEMENT

'Self-awareness, self-confidence, and self-belief are foundations for leading through uncertainty.'

'Pick me,' the horse seemed to be saying.

I had gone to see a horse called Gio, and my eyes were drawn to the large black horse in the stable at the end. His eyes locked onto mine, and I hoped it would be him. The yard owner, Julie, led me down the yard and the beautiful black horse was indeed Gio. I entered his stable. His heart was racing with anxiety, and he was trying to hold it all together. I wasn't sure he was suitable to work with me and my clients. I didn't want an anxious horse. My horses need to be confident because clients are often anxious when they arrive.

I looked Gio in the eye and felt the depth of his connection as he drew me in. My heart desperately wanted to say, 'Yes, I'll take him', but my head overruled my emotion because I couldn't risk taking on an anxious horse. I already had a horse called Tiffin who gets overwhelmed with anxious clients. It was too big a risk. All logic and reasoning made it clear that Gio was not the horse for me.

Meanwhile, my heart was telling me a different story. In the course of my work, I often help leaders reduce their anxiety and find a place of greater calm in uncertainty. I wanted to help Gio find his new home so he could relax and be less anxious, and I found myself committing to him that I would help him. It felt like a crazy thing to do to tell a horse I would help him find the right home. I had no idea how I might do that, and I didn't exactly have the time to keep visiting him either. But somehow it felt the right thing to do – there was something about him that kept me going back.

Each time I returned, Gio was pleased to see me. On one occasion, he was out in the field and nobody had been able to get near him with a head collar. We thought he had become semi-feral since being out in the field with no human interaction. I went out with a head collar, thinking that if the experienced grooms could not get near him, there was no way I would, as a novice horse owner.

I approached the gate of the field where he was grazing with three other horses. As I walked through the gate, he looked up and trotted over to me. Clearly he recognized me. I put the head collar over his head, convinced he wouldn't leave without the other horses. Horses are herd animals and find their safety with other horses, so sometimes a young horse will not go on their own. He walked with me without faltering. He had decided I was his new owner, and he would not go with anyone else!

Horses are highly sensitive creatures, as people are. The uncertainty about Gio's future made him anxious. He seemed to know that I was willing to help him, and he became less anxious as a result. I decided I would take a risk with him after all. In hindsight, I was Gio's last chance at life, and he seemed to know it too.

I'd integrated the wisdom of my head, heart and gut and found the ideal solution for both of us. Gio turned out to be amazing at working with clients. He was huge at 17.2 hands tall (approx. 1.78 metres to the top of his shoulder), but extremely gentle. He seemed to recognize that he could trample us and was extraordinarily sensitive and respectful around people. I liken it to a human being not wanting to step on a cat! Gio was a natural connector, wanting to be with people and yearning for a job. When he settled into his new life with me, he had a purpose for the first time, and his anxiety reduced as his life became more certain. Uncertainty creates anxiety in all of us.

Thinking and feeling

Gio's anxiety over the uncertainty of his future almost prevented me from taking him on. His emotions almost derailed his opportunity for a new role working with me. That's the challenge of leading disruptive change. Uncertainty puts everyone under pressure, and emotions become more difficult to manage. This is the crux of the challenge we face in business today. We cannot pretend emotions don't exist because they are a fundamental part of what it is to be human. Uncertainty magnifies them.

My rational brain decided Gio was not suitable as he lacked confidence. It was only when I was willing to look beyond this and try to make sense of him and his emotions that I was able to recognize that he had potential and could grow in confidence. As I created more certainty for him, his anxiety reduced, his confidence increased and he did the most amazing work with me and my clients. Sadly, Gio passed away suddenly in 2019, but in the two years I worked with him he was a firm favourite with clients.

We have historically made logical reasoning more important than emotions. The most effective leaders integrate the two.

Most people have done psychological assessments and used personality profiling tools that identify habits and behaviours. The either/or approach puts people in boxes and labels their behaviour. While it is useful to create a starting point of self-awareness, people sometimes use labels as an excuse for behaviour and get stuck in a loop of doing things a particular way. Our personality is not permanently fixed. We can learn to expand upon our default habits and behaviours and in so doing develop our leadership.

We are emotional and intellectual beings. We have the capacity to both think and feel, and we are at our most effective when we bridge the gap between the two. Most people have developed the muscle of one over the other, yet truly effective decisions integrate both critical thinking and emotional feelings.

Horses invite us to integrate. If we fail to think through what we want from them, the lack of clarity makes it unsafe for them to follow. Equally, unless we establish an emotional connection, they refuse to come with us. The absence of emotion is incongruent and makes horses feel unsafe. People will come based on rank and authority, but in those moments you are not leading and the cooperation is not sustainable.

We saw this in the lockdowns of the COVID-19 pandemic. Many leaders were surprised by the behaviour of certain employees who could normally be relied upon to lead change. The severity of the disruption, and therefore the level of uncertainty, can cause even the most robust of us to wobble.

Horses provide feedback on how integrated our leadership is. They need clarity through rational thought, integrated with emotional connection. So do the members of your team. While your team may come with you because of a hierarchy, horses make it clear when your leadership is fully integrated, following you when it is and refusing to move when it is not.

Are the members of your team cooperating because they have to or because they want to?

The COVID-19 pandemic demonstrated the importance of paying attention to emotions. It also highlighted examples of unusual and unexpected behaviour. Many of my clients cited examples of people in the team who were being 'challenging' or 'resistant' during the pandemic. I asked them to consider the impact that a disruptive change such as the COVID-19 pandemic has on stress levels and to look for ways to understand and support what is beneath the surface behaviour.

As we continue to drive rapid and disruptive change in business, the emotional impact will continue to reveal itself.

Resilience is not a limitless pot, and everyone will have their limits. Compassion and self-care become more important than ever.

Leaders need to recognize unusual behaviours or resistance as stress behaviour, and seek to support rather than condemn those behaviours.

When disruptive change creates stress and overwhelm, it causes people to rethink and reassess their life, work, and relationships. Many people moved house during the pandemic, with many leaving the cities to live in more rural areas. It remains to be seen whether they will move back again in time. The grass is not always greener! When city people realize Deliveroo doesn't reach rural areas, that taxis won't run unless you book them a week in advance and farm-yards are noisier than expected, life in the country doesn't always have so much appeal.

Nevertheless, disruptive change creates a rethink. Are you happy? Are you fulfilled? Is your work interesting, or is it just a means to an end? Are you living your best life? Are you paying attention to what matters? The recognition that humanity and connection are important was brought to the fore by the real threat of danger from the pandemic and fundamentally shifted the course of many people and businesses. Disruptive change makes us stop and reflect on what we really want. If you drive employees to the point of overwhelm with disruptive change, you could lose talented people along the way. Disruptive change is needed, but it must be balanced with connection, empathy and understanding.

Our emotional response is at the heart of what it is to be human: the desire to take care of one another, to build community, to nurture and support, to fall in and out of love. All these human experiences are driven by your emotional responses – your feelings. Feelings create uncertainty too, as they cannot always be rationalized. We've learned to shut them down in business and replace them with the drive for results. With increased uncertainty at work, emotions run high under the surface, regardless of whether we acknowledge them. We need to redress the balance and integrate both thinking and feeling so we can make decisions wisely and effectively.

Emotional judgement

Many people I work with say their biggest challenge is getting people to do what they need them to do. Often they use logic and reasoning to persuade and influence. Conversely, people engage emotionally. Effective use of emotions can therefore encourage connection and cooperation.

Emotions are part of the human experience. When we meet someone for the first time, we instantly make an emotional decision about them. We decide whether we trust them or not, whether they are credible or not, whether they are good at their job or not. We make instant decisions with a handshake. We can change that decision, but once an opinion has been formed emotionally, we use logic and reasoning to justify our initial judgement.

Emotions have a huge influence on our behaviour. When people walk through the gate to meet me and the horses for the first time, they experience a range of emotional responses. Some people are excited, and some are eager to get stuck in because they love a challenge and love being out of their comfort zone. These are the people who thrive on uncertainty.

Many more people are extremely uncomfortable being out of their comfort zone and need support and guidance to help them feel more secure. They may respond by shutting down, reflecting, sitting back, and observing. Often the masks come up, and they hold back. People behave in a way they feel that they should rather than as who they really are. Some people say, 'I don't see the point of this. I don't want to do it. It's a waste of my time. It's ridiculous.' These people are so far out of their comfort zone and so uneasy with something new and different that they want to shut it down and make it wrong. The situation may be too uncomfortable, so they ridicule it. This is also true at times of disruptive change. As people start to feel more within their comfort zone, they begin to relax, are more willing to engage and become more effective. When you understand why people behave in a particular way, you cease to take it personally and can work with them instead.

The more comfortable you are leading out of your comfort zone, the more able you are to deal with uncertainty. Developing confidence in dealing with the unknown is a crucial part of leading through uncertainty. Knowing where your comfort zone is helps you continually expand your leadership capabilities.

A client and Gio work together out of their comfort zones

COVID-19 took everyone out of their comfort zone, on a global scale. Normally we rely on those around us for support in disruptive change. When everyone is experiencing it, it is harder to have the reserves to support others. We must recognize that resilience and the comfort zone have their limits, and that those limits are different for everyone.

Organizations include a range of people, from those who thrive on a challenge to those who resist change and refuse to do anything new, and those in the middle who are trying hard to adapt but get stressed in the process. The group in the middle will flip in and out of being willing and resistant. They may push through their resistance to get results, but may become overwhelmed in the process. When you recognize who in your team is comfortable with uncertainty and who is not, you can support people better. This is a critical part of making disruptive change work. If employees are struggling to adapt, you may need to find ways to pace things differently, or provide emotional support.

When we operate repeatedly out of our comfort zone without time and space to reflect and recharge, we get stressed and overwhelmed. When you develop self-awareness and have confidence in your leadership, you can develop the knowledge that even when you feel unskilled, you are still capable of leading effectively. You can reduce the stress of uncertainty by increasing self-confidence and self-belief, as well as by becoming more comfortable with not having all the answers.

What can you count on yourself for during uncertainty?

Our identity is caught up in the roles we play. If I do a good job, there is an implication that it makes me a good person. If I'm made redundant, I am somehow less of a person, less worthy. Yet we are not the roles we play and the jobs we do.

> *We are rewarded on what we do, who we are, and how we show up, but the integrity of our humanity doesn't change with how well we do our job. The world is changing and people need more than results and numbers. Results and numbers benefit only a select few. Purpose, meaning, connection to self, and humanity have enormous value, too.*

Suppressing emotions

When things are uncertain, emotions run high. To squash emotions and pretend they don't exist denies us the full human experience and ignores the wisdom that guides effective decision-making. Ignoring emotions increases stress and leads to overwhelm. When we make emotions wrong in business, we hold that it's not okay to be angry or scared or anxious because it's 'unprofessional'. All those emotions we have as part of the natural human experience are shut down because we deem them to be inappropriate in the workplace.

> *Emotions have been made wrong in business because people use them in an unskilled way. The unskilled usage of emotions comes from a lack of practice.*

If you regularly stifle your emotions and don't allow yourself to express them in the moment, your emotions will explode at an inappropriate moment in a less professional way. We've probably all experienced explosions of emotion in the office. When horses suppress their emotions, they become unpredictable and explosive, and that makes them dangerous. We all have moments of unskilled behaviour with emotions as most people have not been trained to use them in a powerful way throughout their life.

Anger builds up when we suppress frustration over a period of time and pretend it's not happening. When your emotion says 'I'm feeling frustrated', it's useful information. Be curious – why are you frustrated? Frustration indicates unmet needs and desires. Instead of being frustrated and letting it build out of proportion, ask for what you want. The frustration can guide you more powerfully to make effective decisions and meet your needs if you are curious about it as a source of information instead of suppressing it. The quicker you resolve minor frustrations and disagreements, the less likely it is that they will grow out of proportion and out of control. Your emotions tell you what wants to happen.

What emotions are you suppressing, and what impact is that having?

Uncertainty increases our emotions. The self-awareness required to manage your emotions grows exponentially alongside the volume of pressure you are subjected to. The more pressure you feel, the harder it is to manage your emotions. That's why it's important to create a culture where people feel comfortable expressing their needs, so that there is no need to resort to unskilled explosions.

Emotion is a way of expressing a desire that is met or unmet. If you allow yourself to feel the emotion and become curious about it, you can use it as a source of wisdom to understand what you want to create.

Many people I meet love their job and may love their business, but they feel under excessive pressure to perform. They are driven by fear of failure or fear of getting it wrong, fear of not being good enough, of missing out on the next promotion or being made redundant. Yet they are afraid to be explicit about this level of pressure for fear of the consequences.

Are the members of your team coming with you through fear, or because they are engaged? How do you know?

One is leadership, the other is not. While people may be driven by fear, horses will not. They will refuse to cooperate until you engage them through relationship, clarity, and a sense of purpose.

The future of business depends on creating a culture where people can be truly human. If you overlook the humanity and strive only for results and financial returns, people eventually lose focus and disengage. Emotions are therefore critical to the engagement of your team.

Case study: Client team

The team had pushed themselves so far beyond their limits that they were exhausted. As soon as they walked through the gate, the horses all lay down in the field. I asked the clients how they felt. Initially they all said they were fine. It was a standard response. They were used to coping and carrying on.

Eventually, one of them admitted to being 'a bit tired'. Once one person opened up, the others all admitted that they were under significant pressure and exhausted. Once they had named it, the horses stood up again.

The clients had put themselves under repeated pressure to perform, to the point where they were exhausted. Nobody wanted to admit it because they had subconsciously believed it was a weakness. Many people continue to put themselves under incessant pressure without taking time to recharge or to recognize their emotions, and this is taking its toll in organizations with the rise of mental health issues.

Source of wisdom

Many of the people I work with, from executive boards to graduates and leaders at all levels in between, have suppressed their emotions so much that they do not possess language to describe how they feel in different situations.

One of the first things I ask clients to do when they work with horses is to observe them and name the primary emotion they experience watching the horses. Often people say they feel intrigued or curious. These are cognitive responses, seeking information and facts. When pushed to describe their emotions, people are often uncomfortable. It's unusual for them to admit they feel scared, overwhelmed or anxious about doing something they've not done before. It's vulnerable to be that honest, and people often lack the language to describe how they feel.

Yet as soon as people name how they feel, the stress begins to reduce, and the group becomes more supportive, recognizing that everyone feels vulnerable in some way. Once expressed, the emotion no longer has a hold over them. Instead, they can use it as a source of information and consider how they proceed. Many clients discover that when they are honest about how they feel, the team will rally round and support them. It reduces the burden of having to cope and go it alone. This is true teamwork.

> *Emotions are released by deepening our experience of them, making sense of them and then letting them go. When you give yourself permission to feel, you realize that feelings don't take over – you can have an emotion without losing control and without the emotion taking over.*

When we are transparent about our emotions, we can create what we want, knowing it is informed by a deep desire, not just a cognitive process. When you get stuck in the loop of a negative emotion or an unmet need, it can feel as though it is taking over, but it doesn't need to be squashed either. There is a way of balancing emotions and using them as a powerful source of information.

Emotions last only a minute and a half. Imagine that! Most of us get stuck in emotions for days on end. If you feel an emotion for longer than a minute and a half, it's because you are going round and round a situation and allowing yourself to get stuck in a loop of the emotion. Being honest about it can help release the hold it has on you and is an effective use of emotions to express the unmet need or desire.

Are you having emotions, or are your emotions having you?

The former is powerful use of emotions and can guide you to make decisions based on a deeper embodied wisdom. The latter is where the emotion takes over, and you reach an unresourceful state. Increasing self-awareness enables you to notice the habits and behaviours you exhibit and the emotions that drive your behaviour.

When leaders believe that all their problems lie externally, they do not take responsibility for their emotions and do not change their behaviour. Therefore, the challenges they face continue. One client explained to me that he found everyone difficult to deal with. He expected them to conform to his view of the way things should be done, and when they did not, he engaged in conflict with them. He was unaware that he had a role to play in influencing others by changing his own behaviour first.

We evoke change in others when we take responsibility for our emotions, actions, and behaviours. This requires self-awareness to explore what we do, how we do it, and the impact it has on others.

Change happens when we willingly accept the impact of our behaviour and how emotions influence it. Self-knowledge is the starting point, but our impact on others also influences their behaviour and has vital consequences.

Mastering uncertainty

- Integrate rational thought, emotions, and intuition in your decision-making. Don't just rely on logic and facts.

- Notice your initial emotional response to people and situations, and be willing to alter your view by being open and curious.

- Take time to recharge when you are under pressure, and encourage your team to recharge and recover as well.

- Notice where you suppress your emotions or where others withhold emotions.

- Allow yourself to feel an emotion, process it, and use it as a source of information.

- Take responsibility for your emotions.

- Find ways to engage people emotionally in their work.

Before you move on to the next chapter, spend 10 minutes reflecting on how emotions drive your behaviour and that of your team.

 Download the *Leading Through Uncertainty* workbook from www.judejennison.com/uncertainty and record your reflections.

Provoking personal insight

Are the members of your team cooperating because they have to, or because they want to?

What can you count on yourself for during uncertainty?

What emotions are you suppressing, and what impact does that have?

Does your team come with you through fear or because they are engaged? How do you know?

Are you having emotions, or are your emotions having you?

Part 2
YOU ARE NOT A MACHINE!

Chapter 4

STRESS AND OVERWHELM

*'The current situation of faster technological processing
power fuelling more human workload is not sustainable.'*

In August 2020, in the middle of the COVID-19 pandemic, Chloe walked through my gate for a one-to-one coaching session with me and my horses. As a single mum, she was home-schooling three young children with no support, having just moved house and started a new job in a senior leadership role with high levels of responsibility. I asked her how she had coped during the pandemic.

'Fine,' was her automatic reply.

I probed further, but she was adamant that her stress levels were low. She was so used to coping that she suppressed how she really felt. My sense was otherwise. I could feel her vibrating with stress, but no amount of questioning would uncover it. We walked out into the field to see the horses. As we walked through the gate, the horses were at the far end of the field, some 200 metres away. They looked up and galloped straight at us at 30 mph. It was dramatic and something I'd never seen happen before. I waved my arms wildly, knowing the horses would not trample us. They galloped round us and pulled up behind us, puffing. Chloe hid behind me for safety.

I asked her how she felt. She looked at me, took a deep breath and said, 'I realize I am like a wall of energy launching myself at everyone. Now I know how terrifying that must be for people to be on the receiving end and why people are shrinking back.'

Work-related stress

Pre-pandemic, we had started to discuss mental health more. COVID-19 has increased the awareness of the impact of disruptive change on our mental health. We must not convince ourselves that the pandemic was a one off. All change creates uncertainty and stress, and will continue to impact the mental health of employees. If you want to lead an organization through disruptive change, you need to consider the impact of how human beings process the volume and pace of change in the process. There is a tendency to say 'you are on the bus or not', but we need to support employees in embracing disruptive and prolonged change.

Everyone's workload is constantly increasing. There is a limit to the capacity that the human brain can cope with. You are not a machine! Technology has limits, and so does the human race. We are limited by our processing capabilities – both mental and physical. We are reaching a crisis point of human capacity, and something needs to shift to enable us to work more effectively.

We need to set people realistic targets that are within their capabilities. For almost two decades, the pressure people have been put under has been increasing, and it's time to take a look at what is actually achievable.

What targets are you driving towards that are unrealistic? What needs to happen?

We can redress the balance and find ways of working more efficiently, using technology to aid us with faster processing power. The current situation of faster processing power fuelling more human workload is not sustainable.

As organizations renew their strategy coming out of the pandemic, the volume of workload continues to increase, putting people under even greater pressure to deliver more with fewer resources. Deadlines are increasingly unrealistic, and the incessant pressure escalates stress levels in the organization. In parallel, technology is increasing the volume of information available, exacerbating the overwhelm related to data overload. Many people are on video calls all day, with no breaks in between.

Zoom fatigue is a real and new phenomenon. Jeremy N Bailenson identified the non-verbal overload related to videoconferencing.[1] He cited four key issues that cause an increase in stress and fatigue: eye gaze at a close distance, cognitive overload, looking at yourself as an all-day mirror and reduced mobility.

Many people are operating under severe pressure, with a sense of, 'if I can just get to the end of the week, it'll be okay'. This is an adrenaline-fuelled, high-alert state, and people do not function effectively when placed under continual stress in this way. It also has huge implications for long-term physical and emotional health. While for some people the COVID-19 pandemic provided an opportunity to stop, reflect, and reconsider the future, for others the need to adapt rapidly to survive further exacerbated the pace of change, leading to a mix of experiences that many have not fully understood.

Overwhelm

In parallel to the increased workload, responsibilities outside of the workplace are growing too, such as childcare, parental care, the rise of dementia and an ageing population. These are further heightened by remote working as the challenge of integrating work and life issues becomes more evident. All of these things affect employees. External stresses impact organizations. The two are inextricably linked because the people working in organizations are those same people who have external pressures. Being technologically connected 24/7, it is increasingly difficult to separate work and life.

As people feel continually under pressure and on auto-pilot to achieve everything they need to achieve in their lives and work, they lack the

---

[1] Jeremy N Bailenson, 'Nonverbal overload: A theoretical argument for the causes of Zoom fatigue', 2021.

time to look after themselves in the process. It requires time to plan healthy meals, cook, and do regular exercise. These are often aspects that fall to the bottom of the list of priorities under pressure, yet they have an impact on physical *and* emotional health. Many people were relieved not to have to tackle the daily commute to work and are reluctant to return to the office. The delays in travelling to work, battling traffic, dealing with motorway closures or coping with a packed underground system in major cities exacerbate the frustration that people feel when they are under pressure. Instead, they have different pressures to contend with: school runs, barking dogs, and no time for reflection.

> *Disruptive change has become normal, and leadership has a critical role to play in how people are led and supported in this fast-changing and diverse world.*

The 2021 Health and Safety Executive (HSE) report highlighted that stress, depression or anxiety accounted for 50% of all work-related ill-health cases. The reasons cited as causes of work-related stress are 'workload, in particular tight deadlines, too much work or too much pressure or responsibility. Other factors identified included a lack of managerial support, organisational changes at work, violence and role uncertainty (lack of clarity about job/uncertain what meant to do).'[2] These statistics don't even include the physical health problems caused by stress.

Everyone responds to pressure in different ways. For many, the fear of getting things wrong is real. The consequences are substantial, too – missed promotions, blame, criticism, and potential redundancy. These are genuine fears that cause people to put themselves under huge pressure, accepting the challenge they've been set whether they feel capable or not.

Yorkshire Water, a utility company in the UK, recognized the importance of leadership and the impact it has on mental health in the organization. Long before COVID-19, the occupational health team worked closely with the business to ensure that mental health training was available to all line managers, as well as exploring how leadership behaviours impacted stress in the workplace. Substantial support is

---

[2] HSE, *Work-related stress, anxiety or depression statistics in Great Britain 2021,* 2021, https://www.hse.gov.uk/statistics/causdis/stress.pdf

available for those feeling stressed, with the ultimate aim of reducing work-related stress and improving mental health:

> " In 2008, the World Health Organization stated that entitlement to a safe working environment that places high regard on worker health and wellbeing is not an option, it's a fundamental human right.[3] In the same year, one of the key themes in Dame Carol Black's groundbreaking report *Working for a Healthier Tomorrow* was to understand what underlies the apparent growth in mental health problems in the working-age population and how this should be addressed.[4]
>
> The report stated that it was vital for employers to understand the importance of the role they have in preventing ill-health and how workplace interventions can significantly contribute to the wider public health agenda, and in doing so not only reduce the burden on the NHS and the taxpayer but also support their own sustainability.
>
> Ten years on, the Stevenson/Farmer Review of Mental Health and Employers took employer responsibility for safeguarding the mental health of their employees to the next level.[5] The report went one step further from the rhetoric of the inspirational Black Report, which prompted organizations to act in a moral and ethical way to demonstrate corporate social responsibility. It took the bold approach of recommending that the government set out clear expectations of employers through legislation.

[3] World Health Organization, *WHO Healthy Workplace Framework and Model*, 2008, www.who.int/occupational_health/healthy_workplace_framework.pdf

[4] C Black, *Working for a healthier tomorrow*, 2008, https://assets.publishing. service.gov.uk/government/uploads/system/uploads/attachment_data/ file/209782/hwwb-working-for-a-healthier-tomorrow.pdf

[5] D Stevenson and P Farmer, *Thriving at work: The Stevenson/Farmer review of mental health and employers*, 2017, https://assets.publishing.service.gov. uk/government/uploads/system/uploads/attachment_data/file/658145/ thriving-at-work-stevenson-farmer-review.pdf

Work intensification, a culture of long hours (the British worker has the longest working week in Europe), technology and the pace of change in the workplace leave employees with little capacity to cope with the mounting pressures in their lives outside of work. Employees come to work with a variety of life pressures already weighing on them heavily, such as caring responsibilities, grown-up children who can't afford to leave home, debt, relationship issues, to name but a few. It would be a triumph over reality for employers to expect them simply to leave their problems at the door, but in 21st-century Britain this expectation is no longer sustainable.

At Yorkshire Water we have taken some significant steps to protect the mental health of our employees. We have made it mandatory for all managers to undertake the two-day Mental Health First Aid course, and we have made it mandatory for every team to do a stress risk assessment, so that every employee has a voice. Employees who report being stressed at work or report sick because of stress are referred to occupational health on day one of doing so. We have formed a mental health support group so that employees can share their experiences and support each other, and we have a proactive approach to rehabilitating employees back to work. We also offer referral to an independent consultant psychiatrist and referral to a variety of talking therapies.

As a result, we have seen increased referrals to occupational health and our employee survey indicates that our employees feel supported and valued.

—*Susan Gee, Occupational Health, Yorkshire Water*

Workload, pressure, stress, and overwhelm are different for everyone. It's unreasonable to expect everyone to cope with the same workload, just as some people are more capable of doing one job than another. Putting people under severe stress for prolonged periods leads to burnout. Once someone has experienced burnout in the workplace, it is very difficult to bring them back to the same job and expect them to perform. People are more likely to walk away than face it head on.

Who in your team is exhibiting high or prolonged levels of stress?

Throughout the COVID-19 pandemic, there was increased dialogue around pressures and stress. However, many organizations believed that it was the pressure of lockdown and homeschooling that caused the greatest issues. We need to continue the dialogue around what is an acceptable level of pressure and a willingness to ease an unrealistic workload. Understanding individuals' capabilities related to stress and pressure is crucial to maximizing productivity and minimizing stress. It is not acceptable to continually put employees under substantial long-term pressure without accepting the responsibility for their mental health in the process. We can't expect everyone to bounce back and suddenly go back to the unrealistic workloads of pre-pandemic.

Resilience

With the increasing pace and prevalent stress, there is a need to support yourself, as well as your team and organization. It's important to recognize that you have limits. Those limits vary for everyone.

What's your limit and how do you know when you've reached it?

Overwhelm can tip you over the edge

Unrealistic targets and expectations are a major cause of stress and overwhelm. The increased uncertainty of disruptive change raises stress levels through fear of the unknown and fear of failure. Uncertainty is a key part of everyday working life, and we need to equip leaders to manage their fear and reduce their stress. If you are conscious of being in a period of high stress, it is important to counteract this with time out and quieter periods of work. Yet people rarely do this. They accept high stress as the norm, and this is not sustainable.

Where are you putting people under pressure, and how does that contribute to stress?

> *Consideration must be given to what is a reasonable and acceptable amount of pressure and this will vary on an individual basis. If we continue to demand more than people are able to deliver on a long-term basis, overwhelm, stress and burnout will continue their upward trend.*

People can and do bounce back once they reach overwhelm, but it can take a long time for people to return to work when they have been absent with stress. The tendency to continually push through causes long-term damage on both a physical and a mental level. Learning where your limits are and keeping an open dialogue with your team are essential to understanding the early warning signs of stress.

Stress is not just a mental health issue – the long-term health implications are significant, with many physical illnesses caused by stress. The wellbeing of the workforce is a responsibility of the organization and is a leadership issue.

During the pandemic, many organizations did a great job of checking in with employees and supporting them through it. It was recognized as an extreme adversity to pull through together. However, if all change creates uncertainty and uncertainty creates stress, we need to consider the emotional impact of disruptive change on employees as part of every change process.

What change are you experiencing that needs to consider the emotional resilience of you or other employees?

Without doubt, there will be times in business where you need people to go the extra mile, but this needs to be balanced with quieter periods and time out to recover. If organizations include emotional assessment as part of change management, they will have a greater chance of engaging employees in the process and experience less resistance. We can and must make disruptive change work for employees as well as business.

Mastering uncertainty

- Be aware of your limits and the limits of others, and recognize that they may be very different.

- Take time out to recharge and encourage others to do the same to prevent being under continuous stress.

- Stop when you feel overwhelmed and find a new approach.

- Set realistic targets and challenge those that are not realistic.

- Provide an environment of openness so people can monitor their stress and be honest about it.

- Assess the emotional impact of change in the organization to prevent overwhelm and minimize stress.

Before you move on to the next chapter, spend 10 minutes reflecting on how stress and overwhelm influence you and your team.

 Download the *Leading Through Uncertainty* workbook from www.judejennison.com/uncertainty and record your reflections.

Provoking personal insight

What targets are you driving towards that are unrealistic? What needs to happen?

Who in your team is exhibiting high or prolonged levels of stress?

What's your limit, and how do you know when you've reached it?

Where are you putting people under pressure, and how does that contribute to stress?

What change are you experiencing that needs to consider the emotional resilience of you or other employees?

Chapter 5

FEAR AND POLARIZATION

*'Resistance is feedback that someone's
needs are not being met.'*

'I don't see the point of this, and I don't want to be here,' Simon said as he walked through the gate and brushed past me in the office doorway. He was the last person to arrive. Everyone looked a little uncomfortable and shifted in their seats.

'That's okay,' I replied without judgement and pointed him in the direction of the tea and coffee. Everyone breathed a sigh of relief as I let the moment pass.

We could not have been further apart in our views of working with horses. I have watched clients work with horses and gain major 'aha!' moments that transform everything in their life and work. I've seen how the horses help clients turn a loss-making business into a profit. Simon had not. He had no reference point. He was out of his comfort zone, on the verge of overwhelm. The truth is, he was scared, and his overconfident resistance was his way of staying safe. It was pointless trying to persuade him with words. Anything I said in that moment to try to convince him of the value of working with the horses would only increase the divide. He was experiencing the resistance of major uncertainty.

The horses win people round quickly, so I held Simon gently in his resistance, knowing that his perspective was true for him in that moment. When his time came to work with the horses, he opted to work with Kalle, as people who are terrified often do. While many are intimidated by her self-assuredness and self-confidence, those who are overwhelmed often choose to work with her, as if they sense that she also has the capacity to be extremely gentle with anyone who is scared.

Simon took the lead rope from me and stroked Kalle on the neck. He took one step forward, invited her to walk with him, and off they went together. Kalle didn't challenge him any more than I had. She recognized that he needed to be put at ease, to be supported out of his comfort zone and held gently. He came back with a big smile on his face. Simon was achieving success as he perceived it by getting the horse to go with him. He was starting to move from his original position of fear and polarization to meeting me and the horses in a place of curiosity and quiet, confident leadership.

Resistance

The cause of all resistance is fear, and it is prevalent in organizations and society. Uncertainty creates fear – fear of the unknown, fear of failure, fear of being vulnerable, fear for your safety. Fear is inevitable in disruptive change. Fear makes you say and do things you would not normally say and do. It shows up as opposition, confrontation or unwillingness. It is your body and mind's way of keeping you safe and preventing failure.

Fear has a major role to play in your survival. With the ever-increasing uncertainty of life and work, fear is a prevalent emotion in our society today. Somehow, we need to find a way to recognize it and navigate it. The uncertainty of our time is here to stay, and we need to continually develop our skills to cope.

> *Uncertainty requires a new approach. When you loosen your attachment on a specific outcome or view of success, fear reduces and you find your flow of leadership.*

We need a new way of being with the unknown because disruptive change will continue to create uncertainty in life and work. The ability to adapt and learn through trial and error is critical to our success in leading disruptive change.

When resistance shows up, either in you or in others, be curious about what is behind it. What are you afraid might happen? What are you wanting to avoid? Let go of blame and judgement and allow the resistance to be part of the process of people making sense of their fear or discomfort.

Simon's fear drove his behaviour. At his core, he is not a rude person, yet his behaviour may have appeared rude to some people because he was so far out of his comfort zone and almost at a place of overwhelm. He didn't see the point of what he was there to do and resisted it as much as he possibly could. If asked, he most certainly would have told me that he was not afraid. Words would have been futile. In that moment, I had two choices: to meet him head on and try to persuade him, or to give him space to work it out for himself. I chose the latter.

In moments of resistance and polarization, there is a tendency to resort to forcing people to come with you, instead of allowing them free will to work it out. Resistance needs space for understanding and reflection. This is born out of attachment to specific outcomes and breaks down relationships. Simon later admitted to being resistant at work at times of disruptive change or uncertainty. He was uneasy being out of his comfort zone, and his resistance was a natural response to keeping him safe in the status quo. Once he had time to work things out, he was an active and willing participant and team member.

When you lead a team, using rank and authority to make people come with you works to a point, but it's not leadership: it's coercion, force, command and control. Call it what you will, but it serves only to deepen the divide, erode trust, and break down relationships. The end result is either that people feel coerced and give in, not through free will but through a need for harmony and resolution, or they fight and become forceful in return. This results in stalemate, deadlock, and high stress.

Whenever we meet resistance, the tendency is to blame the other party, to judge them as stubborn or difficult rather than seeking to understand. Throughout COVID-19, many employees found themselves resisting lockdowns or changes that had been imposed upon them. The loss of freedom, anxiety over health and uncertainty from the volume of disruptive change rocked many people in different ways. Uncertainty creates an existential crisis that I explain in my book *Opus: The hidden dynamics of team performance.*[6]

Often clients will call the horse stubborn if the horse does not come willingly. I explain that they have not yet met the conditions that allow the horse to feel compelled to come with them willingly, and the horses won't come through force or rank. Resistance is feedback that someone's needs are not being met, but often we don't see this in the heat of the moment. Frustration during polarization builds to a crescendo, escalating the coercion and corresponding resistance. The more you try to drag a horse, the more it digs its heels in. The same is true of people.

I often say to my clients, 'My money is on the (600 kilogram) horse if you get into a tug of war!' Horses are physically stronger than us, so they demonstrate how force doesn't work and invite people to find a different way of leading that is more relational, based on curiosity, collaboration, and understanding. In our desire for certainty, we often resort to coercion in order to feel safe. By doing this, we make the situation more unsafe for those around us, leading to greater resistance.

When a horse refuses to come with you, the only option is to recalibrate and find another way. Clients discover greater flexibility and adaptability, as well as increased self-awareness, all of which are enormously useful in the workplace.

With the pressure to deliver results in short timescales, stress behaviours are prevalent, especially in moments of uncertainty. People often resort to coercion to get the job done when they feel under pressure. Contrary to what you are trying to achieve by pushing for results, making specific demands leads to disengagement and further resistance and slows down results even more.

---

[6] J Jennison, *Opus: The hidden dynamics of team performance*, 2021, p. 23.

Resistance is futile... or is it?

> *The resistance to change is a reflection of the desire for certainty and the status quo. There is a balance between not treating people as victims of their circumstances and recognizing that not everyone can embrace uncertainty and change at the same pace.*

I explain in *Leadership Beyond Measure* why resistance shows up: 'If you're getting resistance, people are effectively trying to say: "It's too big a challenge for me, and I'm scared." Those people need help to navigate change and still feel safe.'[7]

Ultimately, resistance needs to be met with more space for curiosity and reflection. When you allow time for increased observation and understanding, relationships grow stronger and the divide is minimized. That's challenging when you are under pressure to meet tight deadlines. Everyone will work at a different pace and giving people space to work at their own pace is critical to minimize the resistance and reduce the polarization.

---

[7] J Jennison, *Leadership beyond measure*, 2015, p. 103.

What are you resisting and what impact is that having?

Where do you need to give people more space to work things out?

The desire for certainty

Resistance to change is often born out of the desire to hang on to what is known, understood, and controllable, but control is fundamentally different from leadership. Certainty is more comfortable than uncertainty, so people naturally seek it as a way of staying safe. The desire for certainty is often expressed in the pursuit of wanting to be 'in control' as if it were the panacea of creating success. People are comfortable with what they know because they have experience to handle it and think they cannot fail. In fact, certainty stifles creativity and innovation, and prevents you from exploring alternative ways of doing things.

Where are you striving to be in control to avoid the discomfort of uncertainty?

Being in control does not allow for diverse opinions, dialogue, and collaboration, and the desire for control further amplifies fear. Leaders who are comfortable with uncertainty are less likely to be afraid of the unknown. We can and must upskill leaders to have the self-confidence to lead through uncertainty and the willingness to step into the unknown. While COVID-19 demonstrated the importance of this, most people are yearning to revert to some sense of normality, as if the uncertainty of the pandemic is a one-off situation that can end.

Many organizations have a fear culture, born out of the desire for certainty. The incessant striving to achieve results under pressure has led to people being terrified of making mistakes for fear of the repercussions. Jobs are no longer for life, and there is less certainty about your position. Even highly skilled employees can find themselves caught up in a redundancy situation as companies consolidate and reorganize to reduce costs. The continuous fear of failure can be exhausting and can drain your energy.

Where is fear impacting the behaviour of you or your team?

Fear and resistance can be exhausting. Change is often thrust upon us, and in those moments of uncertainty, the way forward may be unclear. When we trust that we can navigate whatever might be thrown our way, we can relinquish the hold that fear has on us and lead more powerfully in any given moment.

A management consultant from Newcastle, England explained:

With the demise of manufacturing and shipbuilding in the north-east of England, I wasn't able to follow the same career path that my family had followed for decades. My future in work was uncertain, and that was terrifying and dispiriting. In hindsight, I realize it gave me the freedom to choose my own career elsewhere. At the time it didn't feel as though I was being freed up, it felt as though I was being pushed through adversity, and it was extremely uncomfortable.

Fear of the unknown and anxiety about the future are normal responses to the uncertainty people face through major change. Opportunities can be created out of adversity, but at the time people often feel anxious about the uncertainty of their future because the path to success and safety is unclear.

Adversity is an opportunity to create a new future, based on new insights and information. The COVID-19 pandemic created opportunities for a digital transformation and accelerated plans that in some cases were already in place. Those who see uncertainty and change as an opportunity can capitalize on the potential. It still doesn't make it easy, so we need to embrace the fear of the unknown as part of the process and create space to recharge and recover.

As we lead through uncertainty, organizations need to shift their culture from one of perfection and control to one of exploration and co-creation. If we do not let go of the need to control, we become polarized in our views with others, as everyone has a different point of view on how to move forward.

Polarization

In periods of uncertainty, there is often a lack of information or knowledge, and there are multiple views about what is true. Facts become sketchy and people try to bridge the gap and create certainty by filling in the missing information. In uncertainty, we will come to different conclusions based our values, beliefs, skills, and experience. As a result, we will have different ideas on how to handle something.

The COVID-19 pandemic was a case in point. Every country handled it slightly differently, and everyone had an opinion on what was the 'right' or 'wrong' way to do it.

In uncertainty, we lack the data because it is unknown. In the absence of all the facts, there will therefore always be trial and error. This is risky – especially in the middle of a pandemic when lives are at stake; however, the best we can do is make an assessment based on the information we have.

The desire for certainty can lead people to make quick decisions and hold fast to their opinions because certainty feels safer than being curious and staying with the ambiguity. Polarization therefore occurs in situations where there is no obvious answer and where there are high levels of fear. The Leave and Remain campaigns for Brexit in the United Kingdom in June 2016 were both driven by fear and led to a period of high anxiety and polarization that had ripples on a global scale. UK citizens were severely divided before, during, and after the Brexit decision, with information being driven by emotional outbursts on both sides and a lack of understanding of the facts that were at the centre of the debate.

In uncertainty, there will always be an absence of facts and our brains seek to fill those gaps to make us feel safe. The COVID-19 pandemic caused immense polarization around vaccinations, wearing of masks, the use of lockdowns, how each country's government handled the situation and made decisions, and so on. Even the scientists don't agree on some aspects of the pandemic because the facts and research are changing as further research is done and we witness the longer term impact.

In moments of polarization, facts often disappear and debates become emotional. Information becomes twisted and people use manipulation to try to get agreement.

The media often exacerbate polarized views through blame, criticism and judgement, which creates further tension and increases people's fear. Even established and well-respected programmes such as *Newsnight* on the BBC showcase polarization and heated debate, in which nobody is truly heard. In the absence of a balanced view and in a desire to make their point be accepted as the *only* truth, participants debate vociferously without listening to each other. The greater the uncertainty, the more we lack information and the more we can expect to be polarized in our thinking. True listening requires our view to be open to being changed by the perceptions of others by seeking new information.

Where are you polarized with someone and what are you not hearing?

Without dialogue, polarized views create further divide and deepen the fear. While this is obvious in world issues, it is also played out in organizations, where departments and teams go head-to-head, wanting their opinions to be understood and adhered to without seeking to understand the challenges of the other. In such situations, there is no sense of a shared goal but a polarized sense of 'us and them'. The desire for certainty causes rifts that are difficult to resolve without a new way of leading.

Black/white, yes/no and left/right answers are rarely possible or even desirable. When people go head to head, excessive amounts of time and energy are wasted and relationships break down further. The complexity of some of our global issues requires us to shift from binary thinking to having the sensitivity and compassion to include alternative points of view.

Embracing differences

Voicing diverse opinions often creates polarization if it is done in an unskilled way. The attachment to being right causes people to force their own opinion on others, often through coercion or, even worse, through manipulative and subversive means. Diverse teams are more innovative and creative as different opinions are considered; however, the desire to be heard and understood makes it difficult to operate with differences of opinion. Differences in religion, race, gender, sexuality, age, and much more can lead to polarization if people are not skilled in engaging in dialogue.

We all have unconscious biases, and we need to create space to allow those differences to be expressed and understood, without negating them as right or wrong based on our own bias. Curiosity is crucial in seeking to understand. A fast-paced, high-pressure working environment is not conducive to creating space to allow this to occur, which is why polarized views often remain.

When people take time to carefully consider important issues from a variety of angles, they can identify and adopt the best scenario. The continuous pressure that people feel is not conducive to reflection and collaborative debate but is needed to reduce the polarization and fear.

Aligned teams always get better results. Many organizations are complex, with a matrix-managed system that has conflicting goals and objectives. While the overall company vision may be clear, the execution of that vision on an individual and team basis is often less so. Multiple competing targets cause conflict on both an individual-to-individual basis and between organizational departments.

Tension around competing objectives is common and is often ignored and glossed over; this can derail and delay achieving results. Attachment to specific outcomes prevents a willingness to consider alternative points of view. Alignment occurs through human connection, which can heal divides and relieve tension, but people tend to disconnect at times of disagreement. We need to give people the skills to work through differences and stay connected when the situation is uncomfortable. When we start seeing differences of opinion as an opportunity for curiosity and connection, we can stop avoiding perceived conflict and reduce the discomfort of polarized debates.

Where is tension occurring for you and what outcome are you attached to?

What happens when you release your attachment and become more open and curious?

When the pressure is on to deliver, human connection is one of the first things to suffer. The pursuit of targets influences where leaders put their attention and drives leadership behaviour to focus on results rather than on relationships and connection. Connection and relationships are crucial to the success of disruptive change.

Clarity is essential when setting targets to understand the expectations of people with differing needs. We often use the same words to mean different things, and this is magnified further when working across cultures in different languages.

Embracing differences requires acceptance of self and others, even when opinions are different. Check that you are receptive to connection with others with differing views, opinions, and beliefs. It is rare to get a team to agree on every single point in disruptive change. Democratic decision-making can lead to analysis paralysis and further uncertainty. It is crucial to know when to raise a diverse opinion and steer the direction in a different way versus when to have the humility to align with a team's or organization's decision.

The wisdom of fear

We must not stay stuck in the loop of fear and polarization. We no longer live in tribal villages, where everyone knows their neighbour and has shared experiences, values, and belief systems. We work in a global economy where things are shifting, technology is disrupting the way we live and work, and we work with people with different values and belief systems. This diversity enables us to learn from each other by exploring new ideas and ways of working. We can shape the future of work as well as society when we work collaboratively, but that's easier said than done.

> *Fear has its place. It can be useful as a source of information to identify the things you need to take care of, to identify potential risks and to find ways to mitigate them.*

We rarely consider the wisdom of fear. Fear is an innate emotional response to a situation that puts our safety at risk. Instead of squashing the emotion, fear can inform us and cause us to pay attention to something that we might not otherwise expect. When we pay attention to fear as a source of information, we can manage its impact. We need space to process how we feel about things. Emotional intelligence

71

is crucial to reducing polarization in the workplace, and it starts by understanding your own fear and making sense of it in some way.

What is the inherent need you have that fear is pointing to?

When members of your team are resistant and fearful, there is a tendency to drag them along. The focus on the end goal prevents people having time and space to reflect and process. When people understand what change means for them, they can make sense of it and choose a different response that meets their needs.

> *Fear and polarization are part of the human experience and an emotional response to protect ourselves and meet our needs. They inform us that there are fundamental differences of opinion.*

Uncertainty and disruptive change require us to shift from a culture of fear and polarization to one of hope, opportunity, and exploration. When we allow all the voices to be heard and expressed through dialogue, we can create new solutions to new problems. We can't shift from it fully, however. Fear and polarization are flags to remind you to pay attention to what needs to happen next in service of the bigger picture. That includes your needs as well as the needs of others. Fear is a fundamental part of being human, part of the process of leading though uncertainty, of stretching out of the comfort zone and pushing the boundaries of what is possible. We can, however, manage the incessant pressure more effectively, and this requires a new set of leadership skills and behaviours that I'll explore in more detail in Parts 3, 4 and 5 of this book.

Mastering uncertainty

- Let go of attachment to specific outcomes.

- Be curious about resistance and seek to understand it without blame or judgement.

- Provide time and space for reflection when there is resistance.

- Swap control for leadership.

- Trust in the emerging future, especially if you do not have all the facts and information available.

- Worry only about the things you can change.

- Encourage dialogue where there are polarized views.

- Embrace differences of opinion by accepting and respecting self and others.

Before you move on to the next chapter, spend 10 minutes reflecting on where fear and polarization show up in your organization and how you can navigate it more effectively.

 Download the *Leading Through Uncertainty* workbook from www.judejennison.com/uncertainty and record your reflections.

Provoking personal insight

What are you resisting and what impact is that having?

Where do you need to give people more space to work things out?

Where are you striving to be in control to avoid the discomfort of uncertainty?

Where is fear impacting the behaviour of you or your team?

Where are you polarized with someone and what are you not hearing?

Where is tension occurring for you and what outcome are you attached to?

What happens when you release your attachment and become more open and curious?

What is the inherent need that you have to which fear is pointing?

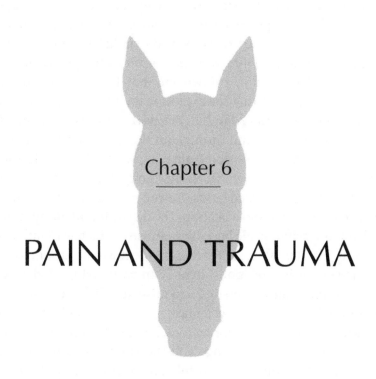

Chapter 6

PAIN AND TRAUMA

'Pain and trauma are part of the human condition,
and our past experiences influence our leadership
on a day-to-day basis.'

Tiffin reared up, his eyes wild in fear and his legs flailing high above my head. My heart rate shot up, and I jumped back to avoid being kicked. The rope snapped as Tiffin pulled away from the fence and he was free. He charged off down the yard towards the gate into the field, his head high, snorting in terror. I followed him cautiously, terrified of being trampled or kicked.

Tiffin stood at the gate, and I took hold of the lead rope. His heart was racing, and mine mirrored his, each of us fearing for our safety. I'm no match for a 600 kilogram horse who has lost all sense of reason, especially when my heart is pounding and I'm overwhelmed too. He danced on his toes, snorting, and blowing hard. I couldn't remove his head collar when he was in this state, so I unclipped the lead rope, opened the gate and let him go. He needed to move his feet and be free, and I needed to bring my heart rate down so I could be more resourceful. Within a few minutes, Tiffin was calm again as the perceived danger and fear subsided. I calmed down too, but I remained cautious in handling him, knowing that the explosion could return another day.

This was the first time Tiffin had behaved in this way. He had been with me for six months, and throughout that time he had been sweet, gentle, and willing. He was doing amazing work with clients and was engaged with me in between. I'd always thought he was easy to handle until that day when I realized he was more complex. His willingness was learned behaviour to avoid a beating. The day he found his opinion and exploded was terrifying. He became aggressive for a few months, physically using his 700 kilograms of weight to shove me around. He had no idea how to be in a relationship built on partnership. He'd only ever been the victim or the aggressor. I had mistaken Tiffin's compliance for willingness when in fact it was a mask for fear. Fear of having a voice, fear of getting it wrong in case he took another beating. Fear of articulating his needs, fear of change and therefore tolerating everything that was expected until he could tolerate no more. Just like millions of people in organizations. People often express their horror at how anyone could beat a horse. But we emotionally beat people down and retraumatize them in organizations every day.

For several months, Tiffin continued to be aggressive, and I pulled him from client work. I considered moving him on to someone who could handle him as his aggression was triggering my fear too, then I realized he had been sold every year for four years before he came to me. He had probably recreated the same pattern with everyone. I had to help him end it.

I brought him into his stable and sat on the floor. I knew I had to trust that he didn't intend to hurt me. He looked at me, concerned. By making myself vulnerable on the floor, he seemed to understand that I wasn't the aggressor. I told him that the pattern had to end – either he needed to work with me or I would put him to sleep. I'm sure he didn't understand the words, but something changed that day, He started to communicate with me in a way that was not explosive. He started to pull a face when he didn't like something. I'd see it and stop whatever I was doing. We began to find a partnership based on trust.

Tiffin took two years to learn to fully trust again. Now he communicates clearly without getting to the point of panic, and I look out for him when working with clients to make sure he doesn't hit overwhelm.

Triggering learned behaviours

At every moment, there will be people in your organization who are suffering with mental health issues, loss, or grief, and people who have physical injuries, disabilities, or medical issues such as heart failure or cancer. These things affect our leadership. We can't leave all that behind. If you are in the midst of loss or have severe back pain, or you have a parent with dementia or a child with cancer, you can't expect to operate at your peak performance level. Human beings experience emotions. That means we are affected by physical and emotional trauma. It's unreasonable to expect anybody who is going through those things to disappear out of the workplace or self-manage it so it doesn't have an impact.

When I included this chapter in the first edition of this book, some people told me that pain and trauma have more to do with therapy than leadership. I disagree. Pain and trauma have a major impact in the workplace and are largely unspoken. When people feel unable to express their emotions in the workplace, they learn to suppress them instead of using them skilfully. Yet emotions, pain and trauma fundamentally change the way we behave and therefore lead, and this change is largely unconscious for most people. I've worked with many clients who tell me they hold back because they used to work for a bully and no longer feel confident speaking up. Everyone is influenced by pain and trauma at some point in their lives, and it is important as a leader to recognize where it might be influencing others.

> *Uncertainty puts us under stress. How comfortable you are with uncertainty will determine how much stress you feel. Past pain and trauma are closer to the surface in these moments, and it is much easier to be triggered by seemingly small events when you are already agitated.*

Negative experiences, both physical and emotional, linger in our memory over a long period of time, often without us being aware of them. They are part of the human condition, and everyone will experience them at some point in their lives. Learned behaviours and responses to pain and trauma affect all of us and shape how we walk in the world. To ignore this in business belies the core of our humanity.

We can be triggered by events that remind us (often subconsciously) of past pain and trauma because we invoke a desire to be safe. If we are unconscious of being triggered, we may experience emotional outbursts that appear to be out of proportion to the current event but are triggered by something deeper, as with Tiffin. When on the receiving end of these outbursts, we often judge the person as 'out of control' or 'not emotionally intelligent' when in fact they are operating at the limit of their stress and need our support.

Where do you get triggered?

> *Uncertainty is deeply uncomfortable, yet we need to lead through it. The continuous pressure of being out of your comfort zone requires new skills and greater resilience than ever before.*

Leaders need to increase flexibility and adapt to changing situations and environments without panicking. When events happen unexpectedly, they can be traumatic – for example, for someone who has been rejected in the past, a forthcoming redundancy programme can trigger emotions around rejection. The fear of being made redundant may be greater for that person because they are scarred by the previous rejection experience, even if they are completely unaware of it.

The COVID-19 pandemic triggered many people in different ways and at different times. Some people were solid as a rock when we went into lockdown but wobbled much later. Others went into panic mode from the beginning. Disruptive change is, by its very nature, disruptive. That means it has the potential to rock us at our core. Nobody is immune, and we all have our limits. Recognize where people in your team are triggered and seek to understand and support them through disruptive change.

Every day, you make decisions that impact others without fully knowing the consequences. If we repeatedly put either ourselves or others under continuous stress without being aware of the consequences, we exacerbate mental health issues and risk burnout. The high pressure of most business environments often shifts the focus to achieving results, at the expense of people. This has a major impact on the mental health of employees and is not sustainable. At times of disruptive or substantial change, there is the potential to traumatize employees unwittingly.

How do you balance meeting your targets and objectives, while having compassion for the needs of your team?

Your experiences shape your world

However you deal with past experiences, they affect your behaviour. When you are aware of your patterns of behaviour, you can make conscious decisions about how you show up and the actions you take. This is a lifelong process of learning. The jobs you've done and the experiences you've had, both in your personal and your work life, shape how you show up as a leader and influence how you lead. If you've had a bad experience or a job role that has not worked out, been made redundant or been told you are not performing as expected, there is learning in that, but there is also some baggage around what works, what doesn't and why.

Your experiences shape your leadership, and leadership shapes business. If you have been a high performer all your life and had great roles and excelled in every single one, that shapes your approach to the next role – you may be full of confidence because your leadership has been tried and tested, and proved effective. You may have less empathy for those who've been bullied if you've not been on the receiving end of it yourself.

What past experiences shape your behaviour and impact your leadership?

Who in your team might be struggling with past experiences, and how can you support them?

By contrast, imagine you've performed a high-profile role that has not turned out well, for whatever reason. How does that shape or influence your next role? Does it dent your confidence, or can you bounce back and recognize that the conditions for success were not in place?

With the pressure of work, decisions are often taken to remove people from roles instead of taking time to support them to learn new skills and do things differently. This has a huge impact on the confidence of highly skilled people as they find themselves pulled off projects at short notice, often with little discussion around how they could do things differently. If you do need to pull someone from a team, consider the long-term impact on the individual. Make it as painless as possible for them.

Every action you take as a leader can have a positive or negative impact on individuals. Consider how you can make this a more positive experience to boost employee confidence instead of crushing it.

If you are on the receiving end of such a decision, you can choose how you respond and the perspective you take. You can accept all the blame for a poorly executed decision and let a moment of failure derail your whole approach, or you can see failure as a moment in time where something didn't work out as planned. This is what it means to be resilient – to bounce back from challenges, learn from the experience, and move on.

While your experiences shape your approach, the same is true for every single person in the organization. On one level, people bring with them all their work experience, success and confidence from previous roles. They also bring the pain of the challenges that they faced and didn't overcome, things they didn't do effectively, as well as mistakes they made and the impact that had on their career. How we respond to those mistakes and failures is crucial for our leadership.

How do you support others to recover from failure and prevent it from deraling their future?

Are you encouraging a culture of failure without blame or judgement, or do you write people off quickly?

There is huge learning to be had from these moments of pain and the challenges we experience *if* we choose to embrace that learning and explore how we can do things differently. Self-awareness is crucial to our leadership so that we can use our skills more readily and more consciously. By our very nature, we also sabotage our leadership and career, causing us to be stuck without realizing it. All our default habits and behaviours come with us, those that help us succeed as well as the pain and trauma that limit our leadership.

Case study: Colin*

Colin had blocked his past trauma and had no patience for anyone in his team. He had learned to suppress his emotional pain and expected others to do the same. As a result, he had no empathy for those who were struggling with high workload and on the verge of burnout. He had no idea that many of his team felt bullied.

When Colin worked with a horse called Kalle, he asked her to move. There was no empathy for her or space for her to have an opinion, so she refused and stood still. Colin became increasingly frustrated, but he tried to hide it. The more he tried to contain his anger, the more unwilling Kalle was to go with him. She refused to cooperate with either the anger or the suppression of it.

Colin realized, as many clients do, that his experiences were affecting his leadership. He didn't need to divulge the past trauma because the details were not relevant. Instead, we explored how it had resulted in his lack of empathy, which prevented him from building good relationships with his team. It was deeply insightful for Colin to realize the pressure he was putting on his team by refusing to give space for emotions and not acknowledging when people were struggling.

Colin had no intention of bullying his team, but his lack of empathy prevented him from supporting them under pressure. Since the workshop, Colin's relationships with the team have improved. They talk openly about the pressure they are under and work together to help alleviate it. Fear, blame, judgement and stress have all reduced within the team.

* Name changed to protect confidentiality

Empathy without derailing

We are not machines. We have human experiences, with emotional highs and lows. We tend to forget this when we are under pressure through periods of disruptive change.

Tiffin's previous trauma has left its mark. He teaches clients about the importance of trust, empathy, and compassion. He struggles with clients who hide their stress. For several years, his workload was lower than that of the other horses in the herd because he got stressed more quickly. I pay closer attention to him to ensure he does not get overwhelmed and panic. By understanding him in this way and recognizing his limits, he can continue working.

Although Tiffin's workload has been historically lower, his impact certainly has not. He will highlight emotional and physical pain in clients, a role he plays willingly, resulting in profound insights for them that the other horses could not provide. While Tiffin cannot do the workload of Kalle, he brings something that she cannot. He often senses when people are emotionally struggling because he has direct experience of it. He will demonstrate a tenderness towards those people that the other horses cannot. Therein lies his value.

> *We cannot always measure the input and output of team members with tangible numerical metrics; we must also explore the value that people bring to the team that is unique to them and that nobody else can bring.*

Tiffin shows no sign of trauma when he is relaxed and supported

When someone behaves out of character, there is usually a good reason and it may not be obvious. People are not always consistent in their behaviour because their experiences influence how they show up in different situations. When you pay greater attention to how people behave and their emotional responses, there is an opportunity to flex your style to get the best out of everyone in any given moment.

It's important to have empathy for everyone in the organization during times of disruptive change and uncertainty, to recognize that people are affected in different ways and to help them navigate uncertainty. This is different for everyone. In my book *Leadership Beyond Measure*, I explain how the comfort zone affects different people in different ways:

> If you find yourself stretching more and more in your work and you feel overstretched constantly, you need to take time out to relax and recharge. When people go off sick with work-related stress, it's because they have felt as though they are constantly in the danger zone and have not felt able to take time out.[8]

The COVID-19 pandemic invoked substantial pain and trauma responses in everyone in different ways at different times. Those leaders and/or organizations who understood this provided immense support to their employees, encouraging people to share openly and honestly and ease the emotional burden of feeling isolated and alone. Pushing through must not be the answer or we risk burning out ourselves and employees, leaving a trail of destruction behind the changes we seek to implement.

Organizational trauma

Pain and trauma are not limited to individuals. Repeated change and transformation cause organizational trauma. As we undergo disruptive change, organizations respond through restructuring programmes, organizational change and redefining people's roles. This increases uncertainty and has an emotional impact on the people in the organization.

---

[8] J Jennison, *Leadership beyond measure*, 2015, p. 100.

When a large proportion of a workforce is made redundant, it's not just those who leave who feel uncertain. Change has an impact on those left behind as they reorganize and adapt to meet the changing needs of the new organization. There is a period of uncertainty as job roles change, and people potentially expand their responsibilities as they pick up the additional workload. The organization and culture change as well. There is a grieving process (however minor) for those left behind as they say goodbye to colleagues they respected and enjoyed working with.

Everyone's job shifts, sometimes in small ways, sometimes substantially. Redundancy programmes don't just have an impact on the people who are made redundant; employees who remain are affected and the organization undergoes trauma. Typically, this trauma is unspoken, unacknowledged, and ignored.

Employees are often encouraged to think positively and look forward, meeting the new challenges with enthusiasm and positivity. We are expected to be happy at all times in order to engage and inspire others. This steps over the need to feel emotions and move on from them. In pretending the redundancy does not affect the remaining employees, the old unfinished situation is necessarily suppressed. People may feel anger (at how colleagues have been treated or how the process has been executed), fear (that they may have narrowly escaped losing their job and might lose it in future) or many other emotions.

The suppression of these emotions generates unrest within the organization and creates a ripple effect. Suppressed emotions cause a lack of authenticity, which leads to mistrust in the organization. Those who express their anger or fear are challenged and criticized for being emotional at work. We are expected to move on quickly. Yet stepping over our emotional experience does not cause organizational trauma to disappear. Instead, it becomes the unnamed influence that continues to have an impact, even though it is unacknowledged.

We need a level of honesty and transparency around organizational change. Emotions need space to be expressed, understood, and recognized. This does not mean getting caught up in emotional outbursts and creating a downward spiral of righteous indignation. Instead, it requires a recognition that everyone is having their own emotional experience and an acknowledgement that moving on can take more time. The trauma does not end on the day people leave the organization or the day the change is invoked: it continues to have an impact for weeks, months, and even years.

Any form of disruptive change has the potential to create trauma. The COVID-19 lockdowns demonstrated this globally. Uncertainty in these moments is challenging and generates a whole range of emotions. How the organization responds, and how people are supported through change, affect the company culture and the ability to move forward.

Some organizations operate on the front line and may be operating repeatedly under stress – for example, the police, armed forces, ambulance services, the NHS in the United Kingdom, or trading desks, where people run on adrenaline. Leaders in those organizations need to provide greater support to reduce stress and overwhelm, and to encourage people to be honest about their emotions.

One great example of such a leader is Elizabeth Cronin, the Director of the New York State Office of Victim Services. She recognizes the importance of empathy for her team and she finds ways to ease the pressure they are under:

> “We are at the sharp end of uncertainty. I have to be mindful that my staff can be traumatized at any time. My team work with very difficult issues. We never know what is going to happen from one day to the next. We work with people who could be upset or traumatized. Each case is different.
>
> The New York State Office of Victim Services provides financial compensation to innocent victims of crime. We also fund victim assistance providers throughout the state of New York, and we advocate on behalf of crime victims throughout the state. It's a necessary component of a criminal justice response. Every claim is a person with a history, a family and a circumstance that has to be considered. My executive team and I help the team understand the mission and keep going back to it. Work is never just about processing something. It's essential to understand why you are doing it.
>
> This agency has had to respond to some terrible mass events like 9/11. In 2009 there was a mass shooting where many people were killed, severely injured and traumatized. We

have to respond to those things as well as doing our regular day-to-day work. The caregivers need care as well as those who receive our services. We recognize that staff are dealing with very difficult things and need training and support on an ongoing basis. We cannot ignore the importance of this.

In addition, people are dealing with their own life experiences and trauma situations. We have to be open-minded and pay attention to staff. We do a lot of cross-training with other agencies so that they can seek support from other areas. We try to have a lot of fun, too, as an antidote to the serious issues we deal with. I recognize that people are doing very difficult work and need to let off steam. Our work is deadly serious, but we are all human beings and need to balance the severity and seriousness with light-heartedness as well.

People need to know that they are supported and understood and I work hard to do that with my team. I'm a fast thinker, so I pay attention to slow down, wait until someone has finished, allow a moment of silence to process ideas until they can articulate it. I need to know what's really happening on the ground and I can only do that by truly listening to people. When you listen to people, they feel valued and are more likely to come forward and tell you things you want to hear, but also the things you might not want to hear. It creates an environment of openness that is really needed when you are leading through uncertainty.

Leading through uncertainty presents challenges for all of us and I am mindful of the need to ensure everyone in my team is adequately supported. Only then can we achieve our mission together.

—*Elizabeth Cronin, Director, New York State Office of Victim Services*

Mastering uncertainty

- Notice how different people respond to change and who needs your support.

- Be mindful of what is triggering you and others.

- Be curious about other people's emotional outbursts and explore their unmet needs.

- Be aware of your default patterns of behaviour.

- Consider the impact of your decisions on others.

- Empathize with and support those who may be suffering.

- Provide some stability during times of disruptive change.

- Encourage open dialogue around organizational change to prevent trauma building up.

Before you move on to the next chapter, spend 10 minutes reflecting on how past experiences, pain, and trauma influence you and your team.

 Download the *Leading Through Uncertainty* workbook from www.judejennison.com/uncertainty and record your reflections.

Provoking personal insight

Where do you get triggered?

How do you balance meeting your targets and objectives while having compassion for the needs of your team?

What past experiences shape your behaviour and impact your leadership?

Who in your team might be struggling with past experiences, and how can you support them?

How do you support others to recover from failure and prevent it from derailing their future?

Are you encouraging a culture of failure without blame or judgement, or do you write people off quickly?

Part 3

LEAD BY EXAMPLE

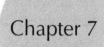

Chapter 7

CREATE THE FRAMEWORK

*'A framework provides familiarity and certainty
for people to cling to and offers some comfort
in the midst of uncertainty.'*

'How do I lead (the horse)?'
   'Does it matter which side I lead from?'
   'Can I talk to the horse?'
   'Do I need to go clockwise or anti-clockwise round the arena?'
   'How do I hold the lead rope?'
   'How fast do I walk?'
   'How do I build a relationship?'
   'Am I allowed to#...?'
   I often face a barrage of questions from clients when they arrive at
the stables for a Leadership with Horses session. My answer is always,
'I don't know. I only know how I lead, how fast I walk or how I build a
relationship.' It's different for each of us.

My clients are faced with the uncertainty of an unknown environment, with a new team, with a species they don't know or understand. What many focus on is what they don't know rather than what they do. I always say, "'You know how to walk, you can see the horse also knows how to walk.' You know how to hold a piece of rope without a horse on the end of it. You know how to build a relationship and how to provide leadership to people.' There are lot of bits of information that are known, even when clients walk into a new environment with a new context. If you focus on the known information, it is relatively easy to invite a horse to walk with you. Those who focus on what is unknown find it much harder to engage the horses because they are too busy worrying about what might go wrong and how to do it.

In uncertainty and disruptive change, the fear of failure often causes people to focus on what they don't know rather than what they do know. As soon as they switch their attention to what they know, they can lead more confidently through disruptive change.

The need for certainty and clarity in moments of uncertainty is great. At one end of the scale, some people respond by asking lots of questions, terrified of making assumptions and getting it wrong. They need to know exactly how to do something to avoid failure. They focus on what they don't know rather than what they do. This can lead to paralysis and slow down the process of getting going. The fear of stepping out of the comfort zone prevents them from doing anything that they don't know how to do. If they are not sure how to do something, they hold back, unwilling to risk failure or their safety. There is a desire for someone else to articulate the boundaries and provide detailed guidelines to create a level of certainty and safety.

At the opposite end of the scale, other people dive in with no knowledge or understanding, no framework and no clear idea of the expectations. They may make assumptions that are invalid or impose boundaries that prevent them from succeeding. They may not pay attention to what is happening around them, causing them to go off track, leading to prevarication and chaos. Sometimes, they have no boundaries, requiring me to repeatedly point out physical safety issues.

> *At one end of the spectrum is paralysis through fear, at the other is chaos, recklessness and a lack of safety. Somewhere in between lies the framework for your leadership.*

Create clarity

With uncertainty comes perceived chaos, as things rarely progress in a linear form. The need for clarity may cause people to become controlling and coercive as they want to resolve the discomfort quickly and reach consensus. Yet clarity and control are fundamentally different. The uncertainty of disruptive change requires us to relinquish control and relax into flexibility and adaptability, trusting that we can create clarity as we lead through it.

Uncertainty and clarity can coexist

Often when there are differences of opinion, people hide behind a mask. There is a desire to belong to the 'we agree' club, yet differences are normal and actively to be encouraged in an increasingly globalized work-place. The very nature of uncertainty means that there is no one right/wrong answer. Instead, there are multiple views of how to move forward.

We create clarity by expressing the differences without attachment to the need for one answer and without jumping to conclusions or trying to force alignment quickly. Innovation arises from exploration, which requires openness and clarity to create understanding. It also takes time – something we often fail to provide at times of change. Understanding is different from agreement, and we can create understanding through clarity without needing to agree.

Where can you create more clarity and understanding?

When you seek to understand what is important to others, you can co-create solutions that could not be considered previously.

> *The desire for certainty means we often seek to have our own view made clear, without allowing others the space to articulate theirs. Part of the discomfort of uncertainty is the ability to stay through heated discussions and polarized views, letting go of the attachment to being right or wrong.*

This is a fundamental shift from the 1990s style of management through technical know-how, and command and control. When you relinquish attachment and control, it is easier to create clarity by being curious.

The balance of certainty and uncertainty

A balance is needed between certainty and uncertainty. It can feel as though there is no foundation if everything appears to be in chaos. There are always people, things and situations that are certain, and it is important to identify them in disruptive change. What is known and certain provides a structure for creativity to occur. In the absence of a framework, chaos, and polarization ensue.

> *The pace of disruptive change makes us more aware of uncertainty. It is not a new phenomenon, but it is more prevalent than ever before.*

How can you create more certainty for you and your team as a framework for change?

Where can you provide more clarity, direction and purpose?

When everything seems uncertain, many of the CEOs I interviewed looked for the things that were certain as a coping strategy to help them navigate the discomfort. In this way, they rarely felt that everything was in total turmoil; instead, they relied on what was known and understood, and used that as a foundation for moving forward into the unknown. They gained comfort from knowing that there were some things they could influence. They would focus on those things, trusting that they could handle the uncertain things when the time came.

Throughout the COVID-19 pandemic, the UK media put the government under pressure to provide facts and data on which decisions were made. They constantly pushed for answers where there were none. Having never led through a pandemic before, there was no roadmap for how to do it. Trial and error is part of the process of uncertainty, yet the stakes were high and every mistake had the potential to lose lives. There is a balance between continual blame and judgment, and taking responsibility. Obviously mistakes were made. This was inevitable, yet unpalatable. What people wanted most was answers to things that were not possible.

Create a framework

Balance and a framework enable teams to operate together effectively in times of uncertainty. Having clear boundaries and guidelines enables a team to be agile and flexible while providing safety and security for everyone. Uncertainty requires a new set of skills and a framework within which to flex and operate. In the absence of a defined vision, guidelines, boundaries, and roles, teams encounter disconnection, disengagement, disagreements and confusion. Differences of opinion may lead to chaos, prevarication, and lengthy meetings that go round and round with no clear outcome and no shared responsibility for success.

A framework during uncertainty helps leaders and teams align more easily and work together. It requires a presence and a willingness from each person to act in service of the whole, as well as an ability to self-manage in moments of discomfort. The desire for self-protection is in direct response to the vulnerability and discomfort of uncertainty. A loose framework that can be evolved by the group enables leadership to flow more easily and reduces the insecurity of not knowing.

Working as a team to provide structure

A clear framework provides a level of security and stability for a team to hold on to, knowing the shared boundaries within which they can operate. This reduces the vulnerability of being out of the comfort zone, and supports dialogue and conversation. There are many different ways of providing a framework – through values, guidelines for how the team work and clear expectations and objectives. The more clarity you can provide in times of uncertainty, the more people can relax within what is unknown, as they have something to hang on to.

In an interview with Sondra Scott, former president of Verisk Maplecroft, in 2017, she explained how she leads from the front:

> I have one 'rallying cry' for my team that is the highest priority that my team focus on. It helps us have a framework that keeps people grounded. The framework provides the certainty within which we can flex. It's really hard to be flexible if you don't know what the boundaries are within which you are flexing. You need to be able to pivot quickly, so if you already understand the implications, you can act more quickly and be more flexible and agile.

Sondra went on to explain:

> People associate uncertainty with fear and see it as a bad thing. You can get paralysed if you don't conquer the fear. The best way to conquer that fear is to dissect it, understand it and identify the worst-case scenario. Then you can start to take action to protect yourself and reduce the risks. It becomes easier to lead once you have the scenarios mapped out because you know the worst-case scenario is avoidable.

A team provides unity and clarity for Kalle

However you build a framework, it provides the clarity around what is known and not known, and sets the guidelines for how we work and what we do.

Empower the team

Senior leaders often tell me that they want their teams to think for themselves and be more self-sufficient, but they don't give them the space to do so. Empowerment requires space and time. It involves delegating effectively and trusting that people will find their own way, even when things don't go according to plan, and even if their way is different from yours.

Employees are rarely provided with enough clarity and direction, and even more rarely given the space to resolve issues in their own way. We need to shift from a culture of interfering when things go wrong to allowing space for people to work things out. When you provide a framework of clear boundaries, guidelines and values, there is an opportunity for people to work things out, as long as they understand what is required of them.

How do you embrace uncertainty in a way that does not add energy to the struggle but instead creates a framework for safety within which people can flex?

If we accept that uncertainty generates strong emotions, how do you equip leaders to be skilled in handling those emotions?

This is the challenge we face when leading disruptive change. While uncertainty may generate strong reactions in those around you, it also impacts and influences *your* leadership. You are not immune from stress and fear, any more than anyone else is.

Behavioural change can occur only when you deepen the awareness of your leadership behaviour and make choices about the impact you want to have on others. When teams have the confidence and trust to give feedback without judgement, they help each other to build self-awareness and develop new skills.

Case study: Financial services company

A team came to work with the horses and found the learning enlightening. When they returned to the office, they used the shared experience as a framework for giving each other feedback without judgement or criticism.

Whenever someone said or did something that the rest of the team did not like, they would jokingly say, 'I think if you were trying to move a horse right now, they would not come with you.'

> *Everyone laughs, remembers the experience and the person concerned remembers how to flex their approach. It has become an office joke that relaxes everyone and relieves tension while giving feedback to try a different approach. It removes any judgement and allows the individual to decide how to change their style.*

Clear boundaries

Boundaries provide the framework of what is acceptable behaviour and interaction, and they are essential in times of uncertainty. Boundaries are defined based on your values, beliefs, and experience, and they may differ substantially from the boundaries of others. There is no right or wrong way to set boundaries, but clarity around them enables dialogue that can minimize polarization and conflict.

Leaders who articulate their boundaries provide clarity and a structure within which others can operate. This creates certainty within the uncertainty. Everyone will hold their boundaries differently. When leaders are clear and consistent with their boundaries, they create deeper levels of connection based on trust and respect, with the knowledge that they can communicate with clarity around their needs. Clear boundaries enable leaders to influence others without curbing or coercion. They articulate their needs, knowing that the connection goes beyond any challenges they are facing and allows them to reach alignment.

Often people relax their boundaries out of a desire to be flexible. Boundaries provide clarity around what is okay and what is not. If you flex your boundaries too much, others may take advantage of you and your needs may not be met. Alternatively, if you hold them too strongly, you may be seen as inflexible and difficult to collaborate with; equally with this approach, your needs will not be met either. Boundaries change as the organization and world around you change, or as you gain new insights and information.

Often when something does not 'feel' right, you may not have sufficient information to articulate why, but the situation may be at odds with your personal values. When your values are not honoured, your boundaries are also often crossed.

Where are your boundaries not being honoured?

With the pressure of work intensifying, many people have continued to relax their boundary around what is an acceptable level of workload. Work-related stress and burnout are often the result of not being able to say no. Unrealistic deadlines and an incessant volume of work challenge our boundaries on an almost daily basis. Holding your boundaries is essential as a leader, and requires a willingness to walk away if they are not upheld. If you do not uphold your boundaries, it results in stress and overwhelm.

In moments of uncertainty, leaders can ease the discomfort experienced by their teams and organizations by articulating the certainty and thereby making people feel more secure. Clarity and open dialogue around boundaries, risks and values can minimize misunderstandings and provide comfort to those who struggle with the perceived chaos of uncertainty. The easier leaders make it for their teams to navigate the uncertainty of disruptive change, the more quickly those teams will move forward together with greater confidence.

Mastering uncertainty

- Create some certainty in periods of uncertainty.

- Focus on the things you can influence and be flexible with those you cannot.

- Provide clarity on where there are differences of opinion.

- Be clear about what is known and not known.

- Set the framework for how to operate as a team.

- Be aware of your patterns of behaviour and their impact.

- Be clear and consistent with your boundaries.

Before you move on to the next chapter, spend 10 minutes reflecting on how you can provide a clear framework to deal with the uncertainty of disruptive change.

 Download the *Leading Through Uncertainty* workbook from www.judejennison.com/uncertainty and record your reflections.

Provoking personal insight

Where can you create more clarity and understanding?

How can you create more certainty for you and your team as a framework for change?

Where can you provide more clarity, direction, and purpose?

How do you embrace uncertainty in a way that does not add energy to the struggle but instead creates a framework for safety within which people can flex?

If we accept that uncertainty generates strong emotions, how do you equip leaders to be skilled in handling those emotions?

Where are your boundaries not being honoured?

Chapter 8

ADAPT TO OPPORTUNITIES

*'There is no certainty in emergence. Instead,
there is fluidity, flexibility and possibility.
That freaks the life out of a lot of people.'*

Opus suddenly kicked the stable door. Bang! He was standing in his stable next to the arena. He had his head over the door, watching intently all morning as clients led different horses. He never took his eyes off the clients and paused only to eat hay when we also stopped for a break. It often surprises clients that he showed so much commitment to being involved even when he wasn't playing an active hands-on role. Horses always work as a collective, which means they look out for each other all the time. If one of them is in the arena, the others always pay attention, and communicate with each other constantly, even though they may be doing something else.

Opus had been quiet all morning, and although I realized that he was watching us, the clients had been engrossed and largely unaware of his presence. As we turned to look at him, he raised his head high and kicked the stable door again two or three times. 'It looks as though he wants something,' I said. That was an understatement. There was nothing subtle about his communication.

I went over to him. He headbutted me, then nudged the lock on his stable door. His message was clear. He wanted to come out. I put on his head collar and opened the stable door. He came barging out in a hurry. He dragged me over to the arena, charged in like a young horse at the races and pulled me over towards the clients. He went up to Ruth (client name changed to protect confidentiality) and headbutted her on the chest. She looked at me and raised her eyebrows in astonishment.

I said, 'I think he wants to work with you. Are you willing?' Ruth said yes. After his formal retirement from the leadership work, Opus was quite challenging to lead and usually planted his feet and refused to move with clients. He required clarity, confidence, and purpose in a leader – someone who knew exactly where they were going and communicated it, balanced with gentleness, empathy, and space for him to feel he had an opinion too. It takes an exceptionally skilled leader to balance the energy of driving results with the softness of nurturing in complete harmony. Opus was a master of fine-tuning!

Clients were often too kind and respectful towards him, and he took advantage of that. I used to explain that if you want to persuade your CEO to do something, you need to be compelling. If you are too passive, too nice or too respectful, you won't be influential. You need to connect, build trust, and be assertive and clear.

Ruth led Opus round the arena, and he was relaxed and calm with her. He did everything she asked, which is highly unusual. Despite being an exceptional leader, Ruth lacked confidence in her leadership and often held back and put herself down. When she saw Opus march in with power and confidence, she knew she would need to find a different style from her usual one. Holding back and diminishing her power was not going to work here, any more than it does for Ruth at work. She set off with confidence, purpose, and clarity. Opus matched her step for step. Ruth learned that when she did step up with true confidence, she was highly capable. As soon as they finished, Opus headbutted me. He was ready to go. As I took the lead rope from Ruth, he dragged me to the gate and demanded to go back to the ringside seat of his stable. He was done, and he made it clear.

Ruth was shocked. She saw how Opus commanded such respect by being clear about what he wanted. I explained that he doesn't always get exactly what he wants, but he never fails to communicate it. It was my job to listen and adapt. In this way, we were able to create an opportunity for Ruth to have an experience that was otherwise unplanned and unexpected.

Flexibility

Leaders need increased flexibility to create human connection when leading through uncertainty. When we pay attention to what is needed by each member of the team, as well as the overall organization, we collaborate more effectively and lead more collectively.

A performance-driven culture often does not allow for mistakes, and this makes the environment unsafe and becomes a barrier to connection. Connection can look and feel very different to everyone, and therefore flexibility is needed to create an intentional impact in challenging environments. One question I ask myself in uncertainty is, 'What is needed now?' This helps me take a moment to understand what my needs are, as well as the needs of others. It gives me clarity on where I need to flex my approach, either through leadership style or specific action. When we slow down and reflect, we create space to be flexible and act appropriately to what may be a changing situation in uncertainty.

Organizations that create a culture where it is safe to speak out increase creativity and innovation by allowing people to make mistakes and to take more liberties in different approaches. Most organizations have created the polar opposite to this. Most organizational cultures are fast-paced, high-pressure, and rife with stress, overwhelm, control, fear, and polarization, all of which prevent the flexibility required to lead disruptive change. In such a culture, risks are rarely reported honestly and become apparent only when they crystallize into major issues, requiring corrective action that is typically expensive and time-consuming.

The COVID-19 pandemic changed our approach to flexibility in many organizations. Employees were encouraged to share their thoughts and feelings, to be honest about when they were coping and when they were not. Mental health was taken more seriously and well-being came to the forefront. There was increased understanding that flexibility has an emotional impact. As we move forward, mental health will continue to be important.

> *We need greater awareness and conversation around mental health as part of the process of leading disruptive change.*

Get out of your head

Where do you have your best ideas? In the shower? Walking the dog? Riding your bike? Running? It's unlikely that you have them in the middle of a meeting when you are reviewing progress against key performance indicators. Ideas don't come from cognitive processing. If you've ever had a sleepless night, you'll know that you rarely solve your problem until you get up. The more you lie awake trying to work something out, the more it eludes you. You get up, have a shower, and suddenly the answer is obvious and you wish you hadn't spent two hours in the night tossing and turning over something so simple.

The answers to many of the world's problems, on both a micro and a macro level, are within reach, but they are not in your head. Leaders who find time to switch off often find inspiration from the things happening around them. Pushing and pulling does not yield results; rather, it creates unnecessary stress and pressure, and slows down innovation, creativity and ultimately results.

> *We need to rebalance how we use the left and right brain functions and tap into the wisdom of a wider system. By slowing down and being willing to be flexible, you make space to collaborate with others, to sense into the wider field of wisdom.*

Organizations need to flex and respond quickly to continuous change. When we pay attention to what is needed in the wider system outside, we can flex our approach and create new ways of working, as well as new products and services that meet the needs of an ever-evolving market. Companies such as Amazon have fundamentally shaped the way we shop, generating the online shopping phenomenon that we take so much for granted today. Technology provides opportunities for new businesses to spring up and quickly dominate a more traditional market. Every business needs to stay focused on external conditions and be able to adapt quickly by sensing into the external environment and making use of the information.

What information are you ignoring in the wider external environment, and how does that inform you?

Recalibrate

Uncertainty offers imperfect choices. There is no right or wrong way because, by its very nature, uncertainty is untried and untested. It provides an opportunity to try something new, pay attention to the results, recalibrate and modify where needed, in both the doing and the being. This level of flexibility can often feel at odds with meeting tangible goals and targets.

Many organizations implemented new technologies and processes during the COVID-19 pandemic. What might normally take months or years to make a decision on happened in a few hours and days. What might we learn from this? First, there is a need in disruptive change to make decisions without having all the answers. If you approach disruptive change with curiosity instead of being attached to a specific outcome, you are more likely to adapt quickly.

Second, encourage collaboration to find new solutions to old problems. Many companies pivoted during the COVID-19 pandemic and continue to redefine their strategy to make it more relevant. There is recognition that the world has changed and business process and offerings must continually adapt to meet those changes.

Third, stay true to your core principles and purpose. A travel company doesn't suddenly become a law firm, but a training company can digitize some of its services. Throughout the pandemic, I was unable to bring teams out to work with my horses due to lockdown rules. My costs of keeping horses didn't go away, so I drew on my other skills to create new leadership offerings. These included online masterclasses, an online learning platform and webinars based on the content of my books. I even held workshops on Zoom that included the horses. My core purpose continues to be to create behavioural change in business. Although my clients could not work with the horses for a period of time, I created behavioural change online instead, even if it was not as embodied as the behavioural change that I create with the horses.

Entrepreneurial businesses create a minimum viable product (MVP), which they test in the market and adapt rapidly based on feedback. As more organizations want their employees to be entrepreneurial, they must create a culture of trial and error, and make decisions without having all the answers. That obviously includes the 'error' part of trial and error, which is the thing many people fear the most. Culturally, if organizations are to make disruptive change work for their employees as well as the business, they need to shift the culture to allow more exploration and trial and error as part of the process of innovation and change.

Case study: Emma Heathcote-James, Founder and CEO, Little Soap Company

What impact did COVID-19 have on the Little Soap Company?

We were fortunate that COVID-19 had a very positive financial impact on our business. As the world locked down, the only outlets open were supermarkets and e-commerce, all of which were our direct routes to market. The panic buying of March 2020 accelerated demand, which left shelves up and down the country bare for many weeks as demand outstripped supply. Producing in the UK meant we had a simple supply chain so buyers turned to us to help. As an example, in one week we delivered three typical months' supply of our soap bars into Asda.

The volumes and timescales were unprecedented and accelerated our growth far beyond predictions. This required us to adapt fast to source new supply chain partners to enable us to ramp up production.

All retailers put a temporary hold on promotional activities and postponed planned launches so we focused on fulfilling the demand.

How did you lead your team?

In addition to the logistical challenges, we had the same team morale issues that other businesses experienced in a remote setting with lockdown rules.

One of the biggest challenges was managing the team's expectations. Everyone looked to me for the new plan when there wasn't one. I had to make good decisions under pressure without all the information available. I reassured the team that we could act with agility to meet the market needs.

Team morale was critical. We worked round the clock as others were furloughed, We tried to do Joe Wickes' fitness and all things the rest of the population was doing but of course we couldn't do it all – it really was business as usual for us, but at an accelerated pace. I took great care to support the team's physical and mental health. I've increased incentives – adding private medical insurance for everyone, increased holidays, and we ran Zoom social and creative activities to keep a sense of fun and connection. Communication was critical and I involved the team in most decisions. Collaboration increased throughout this time.

How did you feel about your success?

Everyone's experience of that time is different. I experienced a degree of survivor guilt [a mental condition that occurs when a person believes they have done something wrong by surviving a traumatic or tragic event when others did not]. I knew we had been fortunate and that not all businesses were able to stay open. I reconciled this by knowing we needed to keep money flowing in the economy, but also because being employed is about dignity, contribution, connection.

To create one bar of soap, many other businesses are involved along the chain from the raw ingredients of oil plantations and freight workers, bottles, pumps and caps (of which there was a global shortage as all had been reassigned for sanitizers) and UK-based fragrance houses, our factory workers, the packaging printers for our cartons and outer cases, our various depots, lorry drivers, as well as my direct team and the supermarket teams buying, managing stock to those in store, selling the stock. My business growth contributed to sustaining many people at a time of great need. Knowing that helped me manage my guilt over our contribution and success. In addition, we had not had an easy ride. It was very challenging to capitalize on the growth and meet the increased demand, adapting rapidly to continually changing goalposts.

Apart from the increase in sales, what have been the biggest benefits?

I used to visit the head offices of 12 major retailers (supermarkets/chemists) every quarter. I've saved 48 days a year of travelling time by switching those meetings to online! This freed me up to use my time better in the business – in 2020 alone we recruited as we continued to grow, implemented an ERP system, put additional systems and processes in place, we also proudly became a BCorp registered business, ahead of our plan. Without the commutes around the country, we have far more family time, and it is better for the planet too. Win, win, win.

We have demonstrated our ability to adapt fast and strengthened relationships with our buyers and suppliers through team collaboration. We've shown the benefit of working with a small UK business, and I hope others will now favour security of supply over price and choose more UK-manufactured products in the future.

Above all, adaptability through good collaboration and communication has been critical and positions us strongly for the future.

Movement

At times of change, there is often a desire to have all the answers. In order to adapt and be agile, you often need to move forward in the absence of all the data. Many people know only too well the frustration of analysis paralysis, where everyone has a different opinion. The lack of listening and dialogue prevents people from being understood and causes a team to be static far longer than is necessary. Someone needs to be willing to take the first step and create from it. I often see teams spend a long time planning how they are going to move a horse. What they fail to consider is that the horse has an opinion. If the team members take the first step, they can adapt and change direction en route.

In uncertainty, sometimes you need to stop and reflect; sometimes you need to keep moving and adapt in flight.

> *Movement creates movement. When teams create movement, they create momentum.*

Once you have started, it is easier to review and modify your approach by being flexible as you go. Trying to reach consensus before you begin leads to over-analysis, especially in uncertainty where the answers are unknown. Sometimes all you need is to take the first step in uncertainty and trust that you can build on it. This way, you can allow the way forward to become more emergent and responsive instead of creating a plan and sticking rigidly to it.

Where are you static and need to move?

Planning and strategy are essential and have their place, but they are not the only things we have in our toolkit. Overplanning often comes from a desire for certainty and can lead to a lack of flexibility. Plans can be altered once they are underway. When leading through uncertainty, we need the skills to respond to unexpected events, unforeseen circumstances and sudden changes, as Emma Heathcote-James demonstrated with her business. If we do not develop the flexibility and adaptability to respond in the moment, we become static, generate more debate without listening and create analysis paralysis. If you find yourself in a heated debate that is going nowhere, or in analysis paralysis, change your approach. Movement is the impetus for change.

By contrast, when we move away *from* something, we may move for the sake of moving. If you are moving before you have all the answers, be clear what you are moving *towards*. Movement for the sake of movement, and as a panic, knee-jerk reaction, can be as damaging as analysis paralysis.

Where are you moving too quickly and need time to reflect?

Movement requires leaders to take a risk, to have a go and trust that they can create in flow before major disasters happen. Unless you work on a production line, where everything happens in a set process, work is rarely linear. Minor setbacks provide feedback that there is another way of doing things. If we pay attention to what is happening, recover quickly, and trust our instincts, we can avoid many of the failures that happen. We can recalibrate in process. Flexibility, adaptability, and agility are therefore crucial skills to develop in order to lead through uncertainty.

Ease and flow

People flourish when you remove the fear of failure. We all have days when we feel on fire. Everything is effortless and easy, and nothing can stop us. We also have times when our leadership feels challenging and clumsy. Conversations feel difficult, meetings don't go according to plan, deadlines are missed, people don't do what we want them to do. Frustration builds. This is part of being human. We have emotions, and we can use them to inform and guide us.

Our best leadership is when we return to the place of ease and flow, without the tension of fear, stress, and attachment. Margaret Wheatley encourages us to accept the ups and the downs of life in her book *Perseverance*:

> It can take many years of being battered by events and people to discover clarity the other side of the struggle. This clarity is not about how to win, but about how to be, how to withstand life's challenges, how to stay in the river.
>
> Once we've experienced life in all its dimensions – good, bad, hard, easy – life doesn't seem so challenging. Every situation is what it is, sometimes lovely, sometimes difficult. Every situation is workable.[9]

---

[9] M Wheatley, *Perseverance*, 2010.

We can make leadership a struggle or we can allow it to be easy. Notice the difference. We 'make' it a struggle or we 'allow' it to be easy. The struggle requires a pushing, coercive energy – the desire for a specific end goal where there is no room for flexing. Allowing creates opportunities, enables new ways, new ideas, new possibilities. It allows for listening and dialogue, collaboration, flexibility, adaptability and agility, and trusts that there will be a breakthrough if you stay in the discomfort of uncertainty.

Where can you allow your leadership to flow more effortlessly?

Struggle creates tension, allowing flows, trusting that we can lead and respond to anything that shows up. The energy used to struggle creates tension and stress. When you find your flow, you release the energy of stress and tension, and everything becomes easier. This is an embodied way of leading, where you sense into the tension in your body and allow it to be released by letting go and trusting.

If organizations want to lead disruptive change, they need to shift the culture from right/wrong to one of exploration so that leaders and teams can find their way to adapt to emerging opportunities.

In the process, creativity will increase, employees will take more responsibility without the fear of failure, and the innovation that organizations constantly crave will occur naturally.

Uncertainty can be expansive. It generates new ways of doing things that may not match your vision of the ideal. The paradigm shift from command and control to collective leadership requires you as a leader to relinquish control, to provide a steer, set the direction, and let go so that the collective team can create fluidly within a framework. If people do not feel supported or empowered in uncertainty, they feel unsafe. The difference between support and control is monumental, and leaders often confuse the two. Uncertainty is a natural part of the human condition, and we avoid it wherever we can. It is easy to be reactive and try to lock down the uncertainty into that which is certain. We need to develop the skills to be okay with uncertainty without resorting to stress, overwhelm, fear, and polarization.

Control and power are illusions. When we relinquish control and power over situations or people, we can step into the skills needed to create harmony in relationships. Once we realize that uncertainty is challenging for everyone, we can provide support to each other and navigate it together as a collective.

Mastering uncertainty

- Be flexible and willing to modify your approach in changing situations.

- Flexibility has an emotional impact.

- Get out of your head and look more widely for answers.

- Let go of needing to be right or have all the answers.

- Keep moving forward, one step at a time, and recalibrate in flow.

- Take a risk, have a go, and trust that you can create in flow.

Before you move on to the next chapter, spend 10 minutes reflecting on how you adapt to opportunities and how you support your team to do the same.

 Download the *Leading Through Uncertainty* workbook from www.judejennison.com/uncertainty and record your reflections.

Provoking personal insight

What information are you ignoring in the wider external environment, and how does that inform you?

Where are you static and need to move?

Where are you moving too quickly and need time to reflect?

Where can you allow your leadership to flow more effortlessly?

Chapter 9

STAY WITH THE
DISCOMFORT

*'If you stay long enough in the discomfort of uncertainty,
you create transformation and breakthrough.'*

Kalle came flying out of the stable snorting in fear, her head held high. I struggled to lead her. She was dancing on her toes beside me, wanting to rush off ahead but paying attention to me as well and not wanting to hurt me.

This was the afternoon session of my first workshop with clients. I was leading through uncertainty, unsure how to lead Kalle, unsure whether my workshop would work, unsure whether the clients would enjoy it. Unknowns and uncertainty in full swing. The morning had gone well. Kalle was proving to be exceptional on her first day of work, and I felt good about the learning the clients were getting. I relaxed as things were going well. As I led Kalle out, my heart rate rocketed as she bounced from foot to foot beside me.

The clients had just built an obstacle course around which they were going to lead Kalle. I was struggling to hold her, so I explained to the clients that she felt a bit unsafe and that I would let her loose in the arena first to burn off steam. I removed her head collar, and Kalle shot off. She ran up and down the arena at a flat-out gallop, snorting and looking out into the distance across the fields.

The clients looked at me as though I would know what to do. I felt uncomfortable. Nothing prepares you for moments like these. All you can do in moments of uncertainty is be curious and trust in your leadership. We stood there having a conversation about how we are never in control and the importance of surrendering to what is presented and working with it.

Suddenly I heard the sound of a hunting horn, and I realized that Kalle had picked up on it long before we had heard it. I suggested that we wait a bit longer, unclear about how this was going to play out. A few minutes later, the local hunt appeared over the hedgerow less than 100 metres away, in the next field to us. As 30 horses jumped over the hedge and galloped past with about the same number of dogs, all barking, Kalle grew increasingly frantic and flew up and down the arena at an alarming rate. It was an incredible sight, but I was terrified in case Kalle jumped the arena fence and joined them. Thankfully, she stayed with us, but she continued to gallop up and down for the next 45 minutes.

My workshop was over. There was no way we could work with Kalle now. She was drenched in sweat and far too anxious for clients to lead safely. I couldn't get near her. Throughout, I noticed brief moments when I wanted someone to come along and take over. I wanted someone to fix the 'problem' and ease my discomfort of not knowing. I kept bringing myself back to focus on the clients, knowing that they were relying on me to lead. I stayed, grounded in my leadership, trusting that somehow we would recover the situation in some way, trusting that the clients would be OK with the workshop ending this way.

The clients never finished their day, as Kalle remained agitated and unsafe to lead. I offered them a free afternoon session another day so that they could complete their learning. Weeks later, they had still not returned, and when I contacted them again they explained that they had got the learning they needed. The learning had been around how to stay in the discomfort of not knowing what is going to happen next and how to respond to it powerfully as a leader, continuing to take responsibility for our actions without needing everything to be wrapped up perfectly with a pretty bow on top. They learned that leadership is messy, and that we can still lead effectively even when we are uncomfortable and have no idea what to do next. My first workshop had thrown me in at the deep end of uncertainty.

Be uncomfortable

Uncertainty is uncomfortable. We naturally seek comfort and safety, and we therefore avoid uncertainty. Many of my clients talk about being in control as if it were something to strive for. One of the reasons people gravitate towards others like themselves is because they know how those people will think and act. It creates a place of certainty and safety. The COVID-19 pandemic has shown people that we are never in control, yet the desire for it continues because uncertainty can be exhausting if we don't manage our emotional responses.

> *We are never in control. Leadership happens out of the comfort zone, in times of uncertainty. Whenever there is a lack of clarity, there is discomfort, a sense of not knowing the destination or how to get there. The challenge is to stay with the discomfort long enough to allow something new to emerge.*

When there is uncertainty, we leave the comfort zone and our default patterns of behaviour show up under stress conditions. An eventual breakthrough is the reward when leaders develop the tenacity and willingness to keep going in service of something greater than the self. When the ego kicks in and we become attached to a particular outcome, the uncertainty is more uncomfortable. When we surrender to what is happening, we can navigate our way forward, trusting that, step by step, we create the new. It requires a huge amount of flexibility and trust in our ability to create the future from what is presented.

How can you be more comfortable with uncertainty?

In the current climate of disruptive change, we seek more certainty. When people are repeatedly put under pressure, they become stressed. While this is a normal response to the discomfort of uncertainty, we need to develop the skills to stay and lead through the discomfort before reaching a state of overwhelm. Taking time out to recharge is critical to enabling us to be resilient. Many leaders in organizations are exhausted due to the repeated pressure of disruptive change. Recovery is an essential part of leading through uncertainty and we need to create space for it.

Disconnection and disengagement

With the increased use of technology, we rarely switch off. Whenever there is discomfort, people reach for their phones as a way of distracting themselves. We seek comfort in the knowledge that there will always be a way of connecting with others through social media, email or escaping with an app of some sort. Distraction is a form of disconnection. There is a desire to move away when things get uncomfortable. Notice what your patterns are in a team when things are not going well.

Where do you withdraw and what is the impact of that?

Disconnection can show up in lots of ways – for example, the moment you get frustrated in a meeting and switch off, however briefly. Or the time someone is talking and you disagree, so you roll your eyes and disconnect. You get stuck in your own thoughts and ways of thinking, believing others to be wrong and you right. You stop listening to the needs of others. This all creates disconnection and prevents collaboration.

Disconnection and disengagement are a normal part of the discomfort of uncertainty. We don't need to fight it, either in ourselves or in others. Developing the muscle of reconnection and re-engagement involves paying attention to the disconnection and bringing yourself back. Fear has a huge part to play in the disconnection. Often people withdraw through a desire to maintain their safety or to avoid conflict. By overcoming the voice of fear, it grows easier – with practice – to be true to yourself in thought and action, and the ability to stay becomes second nature.

We need to allow disconnection to happen, for ourselves and for others, and not see it as a broken system, and to trust that it can be balanced with re-engagement. The responsibility lies with each individual to be aware of their patterns of behaviour and to recover and recalibrate more quickly.

How can you support people in your team to disconnect and reconnect without blame or judgement, knowing that the baseline for disconnection is different for everyone?

When people disconnect, it does not mean that trust is necessarily broken – although people often think it is. Continuing to trust, respect, and build relationships can help people re-engage and feel supported rather than isolated. Relationships require continual attention and connection is not a one-off event. It requires ongoing nurturing, and this is especially important when people disengage. The tendency is to take it personally when you see others disconnect. When you recognize the disconnection as a way of managing the discomfort, you can accept the ebb and flow of connection and disconnection.

When people disconnect, it becomes harder to reconnect because they lose their sense of belonging. If you see disconnection as part of the process, you can show support and stay open, and it is easier for people to re-engage more quickly. Everyone will disconnect and reconnect at different moments, based on where they are triggered and where their comfort zone lies. When there is acceptance that disconnection is part of the process, people feel more comfortable dealing with the discomfort in different ways, which reduces the pressure on everyone.

Polarities and paradox

Many people struggle with not knowing. Disruptive change requires us to repeatedly move forward without having all the answers. The leadership requirements are changing – the discomfort of difference is something that leaders will increasingly experience and therefore need to adapt to.

Difference isn't chaos, although it often looks and feels as though it is because we seek the comfort of certainty and

> *alignment. We need to be able to hold polarities in uncertainty as we navigate challenges with different opinions and approaches.*

This is magnified when we work globally with different cultural beliefs and value systems. Polarities and paradox can lead to disconnection due to the discomfort of perceived conflict. The chaos and conflict that arise from different opinions are part of the process of leading through uncertainty. It is therefore essential that leaders develop these skills in order to work in harmony with themselves and each other.

In 2020, the Black Lives Matter movement increased in intensity after the murder of George Floyd. Social media was awash with polarized opinions about how to create equitable, diverse, and inclusive workplaces and society. Everyone has a different opinion about the changes that are needed and how to handle them, leading to an increase in polarization. Many people switched off and disengaged from the conversation because it was uncomfortable and challenging. Accepting our privilege can be confronting and uncomfortable. We owe it to everyone to face into that discomfort and work with it, rather than pretending our challenges don't exist.

> *Holding polarities and paradox can be uncomfortable, as the answers are unclear and unknown. Polarities provide an opportunity for dialogue, discussion and collaboration, as long as we accept that it will be uncomfortable and that we need to stay engaged.*

We can increase creativity and innovation, and build deeper relationships with others whose opinions are different from ours, if we develop the skills to engage with curiosity.

Where might you be shutting down polarities out of a desire for comfort and answers?

Polarized views can be destructive so we need to continually develop the skills of holding them without resorting to blame, judgement, and criticism. When clients work with the horses, they often discover that the horse may have a different opinion and refuse to move when asked. Initially, clients are uncomfortable because their sole aim is to move the horse. Their attachment to the end goal causes them to blame the horse for being stubborn or difficult. In fact, the horse is very willing and engaged but is waiting for clarity before they move forward.

The horses show a way of being okay with difference without losing trust and breaking the relationship. By contrast, when people cannot get the horse to do what they want, they often become frustrated and want to control it and have their own way. They assume the relationship is broken even though it isn't. Increasing control in uncertainty is counter-productive, and the horses invite clients to stay through the discomfort without resorting to blame and judgment.

Disruptive change creates an opportunity for greater dialogue and understanding around our differences. It poses more questions than answers and requires us to face into the discomfort of the unknown. We can build greater resilience by learning to be okay with differences of opinion and not having all the answers. When we recognize that this is part of the process of leading through uncertainty, it takes the pressure off needing everything to be perfect.

What happens when you replace judgement with curiosity?

Mastering uncertainty

- Stay with the discomfort of uncertainty and avoid distraction techniques that take you off track.

- Allow disconnection and disengagement as part of the process of leading through uncertainty.

- Stay open and trust that people will reconnect and re-engage when they feel comfortable enough to do so.

- Use polarities as an opportunity for dialogue, discussion, and collaboration.

- Seek to understand differences and provide clarity without jumping to conclusions.

- Have compassion for everyone in uncertainty and recognize that the discomfort is tiring over time.

- Continually recalibrate your approach to ease the discomfort for you as well as for your team.

Before you move on to the next chapter, spend 10 minutes reflecting on how you can build your resilience to stay in the discomfort of uncertainty.

 Download the *Leading Through Uncertainty* workbook from www.judejennison.com/uncertainty and record your reflections.

Provoking personal insight

How can you be more comfortable with uncertainty?

Where do you withdraw and what is the impact of that?

How can you support people in your team to disconnect and reconnect without blame or judgement, knowing that the baseline for disconnection is different for everyone?

Where might you be shutting down polarities out of a desire for comfort and answers?

What happens when you replace judgement with curiosity?

Part 4
SUPPORT THE TEAM

Chapter 10

LISTEN BEYOND
THE WORDS

*'Dialogue is a conversation where the relationship
between people is just as important as the outcome, and
every voice is equal and heard.'*

'I don't like horses and I don't like people,' Jane (not her real name) said as she introduced herself to me. She was driven by results, and her experience was that people got in the way of her getting the job done. She opted to lead Kalle – an interesting choice because Kalle is all about relationship. If you don't build a relationship with her first, she won't cooperate. Why would she? Kalle wants to know that you are paying attention and listening to her needs as well as your own.

Jane approached Kalle, stretched out her hand for Kalle to sniff, then stroked her on the side of the neck. 'She's so warm!' Jane declared. It was a cold day and she'd removed her glove to stroke Kalle. She was surprised by the warmth of the horse's coat. As Jane stroked her on the neck, Kalle turned her head towards her and gently wrapped it round her in a form of hug. It wasn't just her coat that was warm.

Jane was amazed. She had never spent time building a relationship. She went straight in, expecting people to cooperate and get the job done. She was highly successful, so her focus on results had worked to a point. She set off, inviting Kalle to come with her, which she did willingly. They got halfway round the arena when Jane stopped paying attention to Kalle. Kalle was coming, so Jane ignored her and started focusing solely on completing the task. Kalle stopped instantly. The togetherness was gone. It had become a task and a process for Jane, the relationship was broken, and Kalle had disengaged. There was no reason for Kalle to want to move without the connection.

Jane went back to Kalle, stroked her on the neck and invited her to come with her again. Kalle obliged. When Jane came back to the rest of the group, she said, 'I get really frustrated when people don't come with me. I just want them to do what they are supposed to do.' Her drive for results had caused friction in the team as not everyone could meet her high standards or match her fast pace. Jane realized that she was not listening to her team. She was demanding results and was unaware of the team's need to be in dialogue and to be included in the way things were done.

Once Jane realized this, she focused more on the horses in subsequent exercises. She paid attention to them, had empathy for their needs and worked with them. At the end of the day, she said, 'I've changed my mind. I do like horses, and I realize I like people, too. I've just always seen them as getting in my way, but now I realize that when I listen, we can work out how we do things together. It actually reduces the pressure on me and spreads the responsibility.'

Maturity to change

At the heart of dialogue lies an openness to change and the maturity to have our view altered by the perspectives of others. This requires a deep sense of listening, far beyond the words that are being said, to sense what wants to be expressed, including the values, beliefs, desires and needs, on an individual and a collective level. True listening includes empathic listening, sensing into the emotions and feelings of others and tuning into what needs to happen next. It is the remit of the unseen as much as the seen.

Dialogue requires a much deeper level of listening. It occurs when we switch our listening from our own thoughts to sensing what is happening with others, with the environment and the wider global ecosystem. This requires leaders to find a level of patience, stillness, and mindfulness that is so often lacking in fast-paced change. Dialogue provides the space for people to be seen and understood, as well as to seek to understand others. It enables true collaboration, where everyone's needs are met, rather than compromise, which is often what teams create.

Listening to self

There are different ways we can listen, and it starts with listening to oneself. This is the primary level of listening that people adopt most of the time. It involves being aware of yourself and your own responses. When you listen to a presentation, you listen to what is resonant for you, where you agree or disagree, and how the information relates to you. Even though you are hearing someone speak, the listening is based on gathering information to serve you. With this level of listening, you hear the facts and information that are valuable and needed, but it doesn't deepen your understanding of the other person or develop the relationship with them. This approach is appropriate when you are listening to a presentation and don't need to build rapport.

Often, the focus is on the information in the head. You have a whole body, which has massive wisdom that is providing information too. Your emotions create a visceral response in the body that is a powerful source of information and guides you to make decisions that meet your needs. When you pay attention to your visceral responses, you can align the information in your head with your emotions and gut instinct, and have more aligned information available from which to make decisions.

If you listen only to yourself and you fail to listen to others, it can create disconnection. For example, if you have had a challenging day and want to share it with someone, you might start by saying, 'I had a really tough day today.' Your friend immediately kicks in with, 'Oh me too! You won't believe what happened to me...' The moment is gone. Suddenly the conversation is on them, and you have lost the opportunity to be listened to or heard. Your friend is so busy listening to themselves that they fail to listen to you and hear you. They miss the fact that you have something that you want to share. They break the relationship with you by making the conversation about them.

Where are you creating disconnection by listening to self?

Listening to others

You can improve relationships with others by listening to them at a deep level, beyond the words that are being spoken. There is so much to notice if you listen deeply and seek to understand the person and what is important for them. You can identify their values and beliefs, their wants and needs, as well as their fears, by listening beyond the words, including their energy, emotions and the impact they have on you. As you pay attention to these things, be aware of the listening to self that also happens. Notice the facts and information that you hear, and consider how they inform you about that person. Notice the stories you create and the assumptions you make. How do you feel about the person and situation, and how do you think they feel?

This form of listening takes practice, as most people have never listened at such a deep level before. You have probably either listened to yourself and how things relate to you or listened to others and what is happening for them. Now it's time to integrate the two. Integrated listening builds stronger relationships through a deeper connection. It is powerful to be heard and understood in this way.

Jude takes time to deepen the relationship with Kalle and Tiffin

The ability to listen at this level is even more important (and often overlooked) when there is conflict. That is the time when you may focus on appeasing someone or fighting for your rights. Usually, in conflict, people pay attention to their own needs, increasing the disconnection and causing the relationship to break down further. We need to collaborate through differences of opinion and include cultural differences in the decision-making. That requires you to listen deeply to yourself and respect your opinions, views, thoughts, and feelings, while also listening to others and respecting their opinions, views, thoughts, and feelings – even when they may be vastly different from your own. This is true mutual respect, in which everyone's needs are met. I cover this in more detail in my book *Leadership Beyond Measure*.

Case study: John*

John stood in the arena with Tiffin, who was running loose. John asked Tiffin to move away from him. Tiffin took off round the arena with explosive energy, bucking and rearing. John had no idea that his energy was so strong. He had freaked Tiffin out with his mere presence and driven him instantly to a place of fear. I asked John to drop his energy and help Tiffin calm down. John dropped his energy and Tiffin stopped.

For the next few minutes, Tiffin alternated between the extremes of being explosive and not moving, depending on John's energy. Finally, John stabilized his energy and found a place of flow without fear. Tiffin moved calmly around the arena, matching John step for step. They had found a place of connection and harmony.

Afterwards, John explained, 'I thought people knew that I cared about them.' His team said that they did, but that they also experienced his leadership as on or off and that they were often afraid to speak their truth. John was horrified. 'Why didn't you tell me?'

'I was afraid you would not listen,' came the reply.

* Name changed to protect confidentiality

When leading disruptive change, there is a tendency to focus on achieving results at the expense of relationships. By listening to and integrating the needs of everyone, you can develop solutions in harmony with others and are less likely to experience resistance if you listen to the needs of others. Relationships transform when you articulate your own needs as well as truly listening to the needs of others and find ways to integrate both without compromise.

Where can you listen to others more?

Colin D. Smith, aka The Listener, works with executives and leaders to develop the subtle art of listening. He advocates that learning to listen is like going to the gym – if you expect results in the first week, you've missed the point. Learning to listen is a long-term practice that exponentially improves the way people work together.

> " Listening is an art, a skill and a discipline, and therefore requires a subtle long-term approach. Learning to listen is like going to the gym. For the first few weeks of regular attendance, nothing seems to change, then you start to climb the stairs two at a time, stand taller, and feel more confident. So it is with listening.
>
> The first step is to accept that you may not listen as well as you could, then to understand the differences between hearing and listening, the practical elements of listening, and finally to begin putting these into practice, by being a listener.
>
> Initially the changes seem small, and it is easy to give up on developing listening as a skill. Those who persevere rarely see listening as a big change, rather a decision that they make to develop the skill of listening, slowly and sustainably. Feedback from clients indicates that the impact of their listening grows exponentially as the discipline grows stronger. Their meetings become less frenetic, shorter, and more engaging. Their conversations are more thoughtful, of a higher quality, go deeper, feel energizing, and so much more – all from simply learning to listen. The more we listen to others, the

more likely they are to listen to us and the more easily we can engage in dialogue.

For one executive, it all stemmed from a simple exercise where he could both see and feel the impact of his behaviour of physically and emotionally dropping out of a conversation. He realized he had not been listening. In fact, he was barely even hearing his colleagues. He also realized the same behaviour was happening at home with his wife and their young children. He vowed at that moment to change the way he would listen to those in his team.

The first 'muscle' he developed was an intention to listen as many times as possible. He started to notice when he faced the person speaking and was fully present with them. He removed all the distractions that created disconnection – his mobile, TV, tablet, etc. He made an effort to be curious and interested. He noticed that when he started to formulate his response, he had stopped listening. He remained silent, did not interrupt, and let the person finish speaking. He became curious about what else they might say and quietly asked, 'What more?'

The change in the way people responded to him was profound. They seemed happier, more engaged, and more trusting. He explained that they felt heard, valued, trusted, and that they mattered. It transformed his leadership.

PWC's annual global CEO survey 2016 identified that '55% of CEOs are concerned about a lack of trust in business today' and that "a high level of trust makes employees more committed to staying with the company, partners are more willing to collaborate and investors more prepared to entrust stewardship of their funding".[10]

---

[10] PWC, Annual CEO Survey: Redefining business success in a changing world, 2016, www.pwc.com/gx/en/ceo-survey/2016/landing-page/pwc-19th-annual-global-ceo-survey.pdf

Listening is the foundation to building trust and the 2017 Edelman Trust Barometer Report highlighted that 'companies need to be deeply listening to *and* engaging with their workforces to strategically shape the future of their business.'[11]

—*Colin D. Smith, aka The Listener*

Listening to the environment

Most people stop at listening to self and others, but there is more information you can include in your listening and leadership. Listening to the environment isn't limited to hearing; it involves feeling into the energy and emotion, and sensing into the atmosphere. For example, you may sense tension in a meeting where there are disagreements or conflict. Or you may notice the temperature in a room and observe that a warm room causes the energy of the people in the room to dip. You may also notice when some people disconnect in moments of tension while others engage more forcefully to have their voice heard. This affects the mood of the room and can provide information on what is needed to create a positive outcome for the overall team, and for the collective goals and objectives.

At this level of listening, you can see who is engaged and disengaged, and how to bring the whole team together.

As a leader, your role is to notice what needs to happen next. What is the powerful leadership action that you can take based on all the information you have – by listening to self, to others and to the environment?

Does someone need to be invited to share their opinion and be given the space to do so? How can you create a safe space for that to happen?

What information in the environment are you ignoring?

---

[11] 2017 Edelman Trust Barometer: Crisis Communications www.edelman. com/post/trust-barometer-crisis-communications

In any group, there will be different opinions or voices. Pay attention to those who don't speak up. They may be afraid to speak to something that they feel is not likely to be well received, or they may negate their opinion by believing they are the only one who thinks or feels that way. Every voice in the system is important. Often we hold back from having difficult conversations in order to avoid conflict, yet the situation has an impact even when it is unspoken. By listening to what is truly going on beyond the words, you can voice what is happening and create an environment of openness and transparency.

What needs to be voiced in your system?

Horses invite us to pay attention at this level. As herd animals whose safety is constantly under threat from predators, horses have learned to pay attention to the environment. They miss nothing. Every fox that appears, every leaf that blows in the wind could have an impact on their safety. Horses are often considered unpredictable by humans who don't afford the same level of listening to the environment. If you've ever been surprised by something that you didn't see coming, it may be because you were not paying attention to the bigger picture. If you miss the subtle signs, you'll constantly be surprised by things that happen or by things people say and do. We need to continually switch our attention between listening to self, others, and the environment.

Working with horses enables people to develop this skill quickly, to recognize that the wider system has an impact, and to include it in the conversation. Once you have learned the importance of focusing on the task, the facts and information, your internal dialogue, the relationship, and the environment, you can start to balance how you listen in the workplace and how you include all elements of information.

In uncertainty, we often lack information on which to base decisions, leading to polarized views. When you listen at a deeper level, you discover a wealth of information based on different perspectives and experience, all of which can assist in making a more informed decision. Dialogue is therefore critical at times of disruptive change to enable everyone to feel heard and understood and included in creating the solutions to key challenges.

Space for dialogue

Dialogue can occur only when we are willing to listen at a deeper level as well as at a wider level (the environment). In dialogue, we notice our differences as well as our similarities. People are naturally drawn to others like themselves, which means we navigate towards those who agree with us. If you focus on listening to self, you will find yourself surrounded by people who think like you and behave like you because they will validate your thoughts and opinions. That's fundamentally bad for business as it stifles creativity, as well as excluding minority groups. While it is important to stand up for your values, rights, and beliefs, it is essential that you also make space for others' values, rights, and beliefs. We need to hold the paradox of 'both/and' rather than 'either/or' and act in service of the whole instead of acting in service of our own rights at the expense of others.

Dialogue involves being in relationship with people who may have different opinions, and exploring new approaches together. Companies that encourage diverse teams are more innovative and have higher market growth. Innovation occurs when everyone is heard and feels safe to propose new ideas, without blame, judgement or criticism.

The point of dialogue is not to analyse things, win over others or have your opinion validated. Dialogue provides an opportunity for people to come together and create new ideas, giving and listening to feedback, taking objections on board, and finding new ways around them. Dialogue requires us to put aside the need to win, to have our opinion validated or discounted.

> *Dialogue can occur only when we have learned to listen. It lifts us out of polarization and into alignment for the sake of creating something new. It is a conversation in which the relationship between people is as important as the outcome, where every voice is equal and heard.*

Dialogue can be effortless and flowing, born out of the foundation of curiosity, openness, and flexibility. It can also be challenging when we are faced with diverse and polarized opinions. It requires a presence and a stillness to truly listen at a deeper level and a dance of thoughts and feelings bouncing around to create something new. Curiosity leads to a new discovery, enabling ideas to be expressed and built upon.

Where might dialogue improve your relationships?

We often believe we are in dialogue when in fact we are merely talking at each other in a two-way monologue where neither person listens to the other. Dialogue is an advanced form of communication that can transform teams and enhance relationships by deepening the sense of being seen, heard, and understood. It enables us to embrace our differences and explore alternative points of view that shape our thinking for the better.

At times of disruptive change, there is a tendency to become more directive to avoid the analysis paralysis of multiple opinions. Instead, more collaboration, dialogue, and listening will enable people to feel included, stay engaged, and navigate the change quicker and with more ease. Ideally, disruptive change should disrupt the market without damaging the strength of relationships in the team or business.

Mastering uncertainty

- Be willing to change and have the maturity to have your view altered by the perspectives of others.

- Listen to self to gather facts and information that may affect you.

- Listen to others to understand how they operate and be curious about their values and beliefs.

- Provide time for dialogue and understanding so that people feel heard and understood.

- Pay attention to the emotional field and use its wisdom as information.

- Prevent and resolve misunderstandings by articulating your needs clearly.

- Be curious where there is misunderstanding and let go of needing to be right or validated.

Before you move on to the next chapter, spend 10 minutes reflecting on how well you listen and where you could improve the quality of the dialogue.

 Download the *Leading Through Uncertainty* workbook from www.judejennison.com/uncertainty and record your reflections.

Provoking personal insight

Where are you creating disconnection by listening to self?

Where can you listen to others more?

Who needs to be invited to share their opinion and be given the space to do so? How can you create a safe space for that to happen?

What information in the environment are you ignoring?

What needs to be voiced in your system?

Where might dialogue improve your relationships?

Chapter 11

CONNECT AND SUPPORT

'Moments of deep connection are fleeting.
In that instant, you feel the vulnerability of
being seen, understood and known.'

The group and I stood at the gate to the field and I introduced the horses who were grazing. I turned to Kalle, and she lifted her head and looked at us. I moved on to talk about Tiffin, and Kalle went back to her grazing. As I mentioned Tiffin's name, he also lifted his head and took a step forward towards us. I turned to look at Gio and before I even mentioned his name, he walked over to the gate to meet everyone.

On this particular day, Mr Blue was in a stable waiting for the vet to come and perform minor surgery on his foot. I explained that he would not be part of the day but that he might at some point pop his head out of the stable to say hello. At that moment, as if by magic, his face appeared over the stable door. Meanwhile, Opus, my 29-year-old retired horse, was 50 metres away in a small paddock standing behind a 5 foot bale of hay, eating. You could just about see him. The gate to the paddock was open as Opus used to have the full run of the yard when I am onsite – it was his privilege as the old man of the herd.

As I started to explain about Opus being retired, he looked up and stepped to one side of the hay bale so we could see him. One of the clients gasped, 'Does he really know you are talking about him? Have you trained them to do this?' Yes, they know when we are talking about them, and no, I have not trained them. In fact, it's the opposite. All of my horses are encouraged to be themselves, to be as close to a natural horse as is possible in a domesticated environment, to have an opinion and to assert their right to make it clear. It sounds incredible but this is a pattern that plays out repeatedly when introducing clients to the horses.

We continued our conversation, and I explained that Opus had free run of the yard and would probably want to come and meet them at some point throughout the day. At that moment, Opus walked out of the field and up the yard towards us. He stopped halfway and stood sentinel outside the gate to the arena. We were heading there next, and he knew it.

Opus stops a client to say hello

We walked down the yard to enter the arena, and Opus blocked our path. He stood quietly, commanding respect and attention. As each client walked past him, they said hello to him. Some of them stroked his neck, others let him sniff their hand. They were completely in awe of what had just happened. Once each person had said hello to Opus, he relaxed further and let them pass. When one person tried to pass him without greeting, he stretched out his neck and blocked their way until they said hello. There was no doubt who was in charge in this moment, and the connection was felt deeply by everyone.

People are often surprised by my relationship with the horses. They comment on how connected we are and how much respect I give each of them. The horses are allowed to have their opinion, and I work with them without using force, which is rare in any walk of life. As soon as we revert to force, we have ceased to lead. I invite the horses to want to work with me and my clients. As a result, their level of engagement is high.

Connecting in different ways

Connection looks and feels different to everyone. Some people feel connected only when they are physically in the same location while others feel connected at a distance and out of sight. Opus formally retired from working with clients as he found it too tiring. He typically spent the day out in the field when I worked with clients. Despite that, he was always connected to me and always paid attention. If I mentioned his name, he would lift his head and start to walk towards the gate. This always surprised clients. They would ask whether he heard me mention his name when he was at least 50 metres away. He didn't hear what was said, but he sensed when he was being spoken about, just as you sense it in the office. This is the power of connection. We are energetically connected far more than we may realize. This is critical when working remotely and is a sensory skill that we can develop further.

Each of the horses connects in very different ways. Kalle often connects in a maternal and nurturing way when she senses someone needs to be supported. By contrast, she will headbutt you into next week if she thinks you need to be put in your place! Both are forms of connection, providing feedback in different ways according to what she senses you need. There is no self-serving leadership here. She is leading in service of the whole. Opus connected by being around us, by missing nothing

145

and coming when he was spoken about. He would strut down the yard, ignoring everyone. Contrary to Kalle's way of connecting, he showed little tenderness in these moments; instead, he commanded respect and reverence for his elder wisdom. The connection was no less deep, even if he was not gazing deeply into your eye in a loving way!

Every leader has a different way of connecting. When you know what your default pattern is, you can see the impact you have on different people and flex your style according to what is required.

> *Connection is a two-way process, and not everyone wants to connect in the same way. If someone rejects the connection, it is not necessarily a personal affront but rather a difference to be curious about, understood and embraced.*

Opposites often attract, so everyone will find it easier or more difficult to connect with different people. The challenge as leaders is to foster an environment where everyone feels safe to connect in their own way by bringing all of who they are. This is increasingly more relevant as a result of the pandemic, where we saw disconnection and isolation as a result of remote working.

When clients experience the depth of connection they get with the horses, they feel the power and also the vulnerability of being in connection. Once they have experienced connection in this way, they are less afraid of it and return to the workplace knowing how to connect in a variety of ways according to different needs.

Remote connections

In the first edition of this book, I talked about leading virtual teams and the use of conference calls. In my IBM career, in the late 1990s and early 2000s, I spent over a decade leading virtual teams when technology was limited to support connection. I developed the ability to listen at a deeper level, to hear beyond the words, to sense into the energy and emotions of the people on the call. If I felt people were not engaged, I would speak openly to it.

After the COVID-19 pandemic, we are all familiar with video calls, which certainly makes it easier to connect when remote working.

However, minor disagreements are easier to ignore when working remotely. If you have a disagreement in the office, it's much easier to pop by someone's desk later in the day and iron it out, making sure the relationship is not damaged. It's a more organic way of maintaining the relationship.

In my book *Opus: The Hidden Dynamics of Team Performance*,[12] I explore 12 hidden dynamics that occur in teams. These include topics such as energy and emotions, boundaries, assumptions, intentions, and the quality of listening. It is easier to disconnect unconsciously when working remotely, and you need to pay more attention to how you keep the team engaged. In Chapter 3 of the book, I explain that 'Conversation is the route to resolving differences of opinion, deepening understanding of each other, and preventing confusion and misunderstandings which are the source of most conflict.'

When working remotely, you need to look for those hidden dynamics and hone the ability to sense into what is happening in relationships. You have to orchestrate connection in a more proactive way. In *Opus*, I share ideas on how to verbalize the non-verbal behaviours, thoughts, and feelings we all have and turn them into a better quality of conversation.

Despite the rapid implementation of video technology, leading virtual teams brings a greater challenge of connection. There is no substitute for being physically together and sensing someone else's heartbeat and physical energy. The 3D experience of a human being is vastly different from the pixelated 2D image we work with online. Online working has required us to develop a new way of being together. Having the camera on can help build the connection, but it can also feel overwhelming at times. In the office, you would never sit square on face to face and stare at each other for a full hour without moving or looking away, yet with video calls we often find ourselves doing this.

I'm a natural fidgeter and move my body a lot, but online I find myself unnaturally sitting still to avoid being a distraction. This creates tension in my body, which I've had to learn to relax without fidgeting. While we have all become accustomed to this way of working, it is still unnatural behaviour and requires us to continually be more conscious of how we show up.

---

[12] J Jennison, *Opus: The hidden dynamics of team performance*, 2021.

A client creates a connection with Kalle

Leading virtual teams brings about the uncertainty of connection. It requires greater trust in others. When you trust your instincts and intuition about who is not engaged, you can be curious and engage in dialogue around what is causing the disconnection. Many video calls are an excuse to get everyone together to provide updates, but if people have timed out, there is no value. If everyone is joining update calls with their cameras off, you can be sure they are multi-tasking because the call adds little value to them, or they have other priorities. Technology can hinder or support connection, and how you use it is a leadership choice moment by moment.

What calls are you leading that have no value to the whole team?

How can you increase connection with remote team working?

Build rapport

The moment many clients feel most connected to my horses is when they have their first interaction with them. Even observing the horses in the field at the beginning of the day, clients may feel disconnected and merely passive observers. The same is not true for the horses. The second clients walk through the gate, the horses have a sense of who the clients are, their energy, intentions, emotions, and sensitivity. The clients have entered their territory. The safety and integrity of the herd are in question, and the horses need to be aware of that and assess it.

In these first few moments, before the clients have even realized it, they have created an impact. The same is true with people. You may not be consciously aware, but subconsciously you assess everyone you meet before you shake their hand. You already have a sense of whether you want to be connected or not. You feel drawn or repelled based on their energy. The second you join a video call or walk into a room, you have an impact.

How do you show up in the first moment of connection?

Most clients arrive at my stables feeling nervous. This can vary from being mildly nervous at being out of their comfort zone, to terrified at the prospect of doing something different, to slightly unsure about how it will pan out. People handle their nerves differently. Some arrive posturing and pretending that everything is fine. There may be high levels of banter and humour that mask the discomfort and distract them from feeling what they really feel. Others are more open and transparent about their feelings, naming the anxiety or scepticism early on. As one person names it, the others relax and open up too. Being honest, transparent, and vulnerable in this way is a huge strength, as it opens the doorway for others to connect human to human without all the self-imposed expectations of how they think they should be.

> *Our capacity to connect is amazing and heart-warming, and is limited only by our attention, belief and fear.*

When clients tell me they are deeply sceptical about working with the horses, it opens the door to dialogue and understanding, which deepens the connection between us. We can work through our differences when we are open and honest about them, leading to greater connection. It is critical when leading disruptive change – especially online – to create an environment where people feel safe to voice their scepticism and resistance, to help them stay connected and support each other through it.

One of the benefits of working from home is that we have an insight into people's private lives. As such, the barriers drop more than they would in the office, and we get a sense of who people really are. I was recently on a Zoom call with a client I have known for five years. My nine-month-old puppy tried to climb on my lap and became visible to him. We discovered our mutual passion for Labradors, he called his dog into his office for me to meet her, then we chatted about dogs for a couple of minutes. We then continued our conversation about institutionalised racism and what we are doing about it. The brief distraction that our dogs brought alleviated the discomfort of a serious topic and enabled us to connect in a different way with a newly discovered shared interest.

The irony was not lost on me. On a call where we were discussing something important to both of us (acting against racism) – a topic that is also rife with danger and 'getting it wrong' – our dogs eased the emotional intensity and connected us in a different way. This is how we build emotional connection through technology, by showing up more fully, in a raw and vulnerable way. Pre pandemic, I'm sure I would have shut my dog out of the room for the sake of being 'professional'; now I'm aware that she can be a connector as long as I manage the distraction.

Deepen connection

Moments of deep connection are fleeting. In that moment, there is a feeling of being seen, understood, and known. It is vulnerable to be seen at that level, which is why we connect and disconnect, on and off.

When clients meet the horses, they often look them in the eye. The horses draw you in as far as you are willing to go. The connection can be deep. Some horses draw you in further than others. It depends on how they feel towards you, as well as how you feel about them. Once you have built a deep level of connection, however fleeting, it becomes easier to align through differences. When you truly see someone as a human being, there is an opportunity to meet them in that humanity. When we are in conflict, we are more likely to objectify people, which leads to disconnection.

Clients regularly tell me that it takes months to build trust. When they hold this as a core belief, they prevent connection with others. They often explain that they drop their guard more with their team and connect with them more deeply than with other departments within the organization. They allow people they know to see them. By contrast, other departments are regarded as the competition or even the enemy, competing for resources, making unreasonable requests, creating more workload and generating conflict. Connection is missing from these relationships. Continually building connection takes time and effort and may depend on how important the relationship is. Connection creates an intimacy and a vulnerability of being seen at a deep level, which people often shy away from.

Many people are running at such high speed that they have become disconnected from themselves. Your body is not a carrier for the brain or the machine that gets you from A to B. You are your body as well as your mind. Your body provides information about stresses and strains; it is your life force, your sense of being in the world. It is only when you can truly connect to yourself that you can create connection with others. The horses invite us to pay more attention to our physical bodies, to be aware of where we are in relation to them and each other, and to pay attention to the gut instinct and emotions that are invoked in their presence.

Alignment

It is important to stay connected through differences of opinion. There is a tendency to withdraw from people you disagree with as a form of self-protection, and it's easier to do so online. We need a clarity of purpose to align in uncertainty, to ensure we stay true to our vision and purpose. Disruptive change creates polarized opinions and requires a proactive approach to finding alignment through those differences of opinion.

Where are you not aligned and how can you create that alignment?

People think they are aligned, but they often use the same language to mean different things. Tension is created when people do not deliver as you would expect them to deliver, often based on misunderstandings over what appear to be obvious things. Be open and curious, take time to listen, and engage in dialogue to rebuild connection.

Laurel Dines, former HR Director for Hudson Talent Solutions, was amazed by how quickly the horses responded to what people were thinking and feeling. She discovered key insights that she has been able to take back to the boardroom to improve the way the team connects:

> "There were four of us trying to lead a horse around an obstacle course, something you would think was really simple. However, although we knew what we wanted to do and had in part discussed tactics, it soon became very clear that we all had different ideas of how to do it. When the horse did not respond, it was frustrating. We thought we were agreed and had a shared purpose, but we were disjointed in our approach and this confused the horse to the state of inaction. Once the horse stopped, getting back on track was really difficult.
>
> It brought home to me how often this lack of alignment happens in the workplace and why we are then surprised and frustrated that nothing changes. We look for excuses – 'it's them, not us' – but direct feedback from a horse is unavoidable. It's not offensive, it's just fact, and you have to change your approach or nothing happens.
>
> I've been on umpteen team-building events, but this was different. This beautiful horse is just standing, refusing to move until you get aligned as a team. That feeling when you ask the horse to come with you, and they do, is magical. It really brought home that this is how we need to work with people in the workplace as well. It's so powerful.
>
> When we go at 120 miles per hour, we don't spend enough time building the connection with people. We need to slow down, make time to connect and build the relationship, otherwise everything suffers.
>
> —*Laurel Dines, former HR Director, Hudson Talent Solutions*

Disruptive change can create disconnection at a time when teams most need to support each other. With polarized opinions and resistance to change being common, employees disengage and disconnect easily if they don't feel included in the decision-making process. More focus and attention to supporting employees in embracing the uncertainty of change is critical to leading disruptive change.

Mastering uncertainty

- Explore how others connect in different ways.

- Foster an environment where everyone feels safe to connect in their own way, by bringing all of themselves.

- Notice where you use technology to distract or disconnect.

- Notice where others disconnect and invite them to re-engage.

- Stay connected through differences of opinion and avoid the need to withdraw for self-protection.

- Clarify what you mean and understand to ensure alignment.

- Slow down and take time to connect and build relationships.

Before you move on to the next chapter, spend 10 minutes reflecting on how you connect with others and where you could deepen the relationship to support others better.

 Download the *Leading Through Uncertainty* workbook from www.judejennison.com/uncertainty and record your reflections.

Provoking personal insight

What calls are you leading that have no value to the whole team?

How can you increase connection with remote team working?

How do you show up in the first moment of connection?

Where are you not aligned and how can you create that alignment?

Chapter 12

BUILD TRUST

'You can build trust in an instant, and you can break it in an instant, too. Trust is a leadership choice.'

Gio walked calmly off the horse lorry and stood with his head held high, surveying the environment. How would he integrate with the rest of the herd? It was uncertain – both for him and me. I badly wanted him to integrate without a hitch. There was a lot riding on this moment!

As a prey animal, it is stressful for horses to move to a new yard. Their safety depends on their ability to integrate into the herd. I had no reference for how Gio would behave. He walked calmly off the lorry, trusting me and trusting himself. He was vulnerable. He could have panicked and tried to retreat, but that would have rendered him less safe. It may be counter-intuitive, but Gio created his safety through trust and vulnerability.

His sense of calm as he stepped off the lorry helped me to trust him in return. We built mutual trust in that instant, as I realized he would not throw his 700 kilograms of weight about. I also trusted in my horsemanship and leadership capabilities. I knew that I could handle him if he panicked. My calm sense of trust provided an environment for Gio to relax into. We co-created trust, both being vulnerable in the process.

Tiffin and Kalle stood in the field at the end of the paddock watching from the other side of the gate. Gio sensed that he needed to win them over. He walked calmly and confidently down the paddock towards them, past Mr Blue and Opus on the other side of the fence. Tiffin grew as tall as he could as Gio approached. I was thankful the gate was between them as I watched to see what would happen. Gio walked over to Tiffin at the gate and dropped his head to the floor to show he was no threat. He was building trust and respect. Tiffin stood still, taken aback. He had been ready for a fight. He dropped his head to the floor as well, and they sniffed each other through the gate. The first meeting had gone well, albeit with the safety of separate paddocks.

Three days later, I stood watching the horses. It was a scorching hot day. With the sun beating down, all the horses were dozing calmly with their eyes half-closed. Was it too soon to integrate Gio into the herd?

The previous horse to arrive on my yard had not integrated well. He had been dominant and aggressive in the herd as well as with my human team, and he had left the yard a year later, leaving everyone exhausted. It had been a challenging process that created stress for me and my team (horse and human). Now here was Gio attempting to integrate. I desperately didn't want to put my equine herd or human team through a similar experience. I had a choice – to trust that Gio was different or to be anxious about his integration into the herd. I chose to trust him.

I opened the gate, feeling slightly nervous. I didn't want anyone to be injured. I had to trust that Gio would show sensitivity to the herd, trust that the rest of the herd would not hurt him and trust that if I needed to separate him again, I could step into the herd and do that safely. By being calm and trusting Gio, I created an environment for him to relax further.

Gio was skilful in how he moved towards the herd and moved away again when he felt he was too close. He sensed into what the herd needed, continuing to edge nearer over the coming days until within a week he was fully integrated. There was no ego, no jostling for position, just a continuous ebb and flow of movement as he gradually built a foundation of trust and became a valued member of the herd.

Trust is a leadership choice

Trust is a choice

Trust is a leadership choice. There is a long-held myth that trust can take months to build. It starts from the moment you trust yourself and your leadership capabilities. Only then can you trust others.

When you start a new job in a new company, you are out of your comfort zone and your body becomes more alert as you work out how to manage your safety in a new environment. Who can you trust? Who will help you? How can you show your capabilities and be true to yourself? Is it okay to be vulnerable? When we lead through uncertainty, these are the questions that subconsciously determine our behaviour. We make decisions and choices based on the limited available information. Logic, cognitive processing, and reasoning don't really help here. It ultimately comes down to self-confidence and self-belief in your abilities.

Self-awareness is a crucial part of trusting yourself. If you know what your leadership qualities are, you can stand strongly in your position, no matter how much uncertainty there is. You can count on yourself for those qualities. I know for certain that I act with courage and compassion. These are two qualities that are unquestioningly inherent in my leadership, regardless of the situation. It means that in moments of uncertainty and doubt, I have some certainty about my leadership because I trust in my ability to be courageous and compassionate in every given moment. They form part of my framework in uncertainty.

Which qualities are inherent in your leadership?

> *There is no certainty with trust. It is something you feel. You have to take a leap of faith to trust someone, but somebody has to take that first step. We can choose to trust when we have self-confidence in our abilities.*

Trust is more difficult during uncertainty. The desire to be safe and secure determines behaviour, and we often seek to protect ourselves. As a species, we are not likely to be at risk of being eaten by a tiger, but our primal responses cause us to behave in uncertainty as if we were. Everything seems to threaten our safety. Trust is an unquestioning assumption that we can create our safety. It is often focused on external interactions, but it starts with self. Leaders who trust themselves first feel more confident in creating trust with others.

Where are you not trusting yourself?

Who else are you not trusting?

Who in your team is struggling to trust in uncertainty?

When clients arrive at my stables, they are nervous, unsure about whether they can lead a horse and terrified of making fools of themselves. The uncertainty they feel is immense, and uncertainty can erode trust quickly and easily if we allow it to. In the first few moments of the day, I establish trust with my clients. As a leader, I take responsibility for helping people who feel vulnerable to feel at ease. I am open and transparent, which helps them trust me quickly. I put aside my own vulnerability and trust that clients will get great learning, even those who seem highly resistant and vocal about it at the beginning. I trust that I can provide a great experience for them, even if they don't believe it and their behaviour indicates otherwise at the beginning. Every action I take is based on these assumptions of trust, which means I act with integrity and do my best work. I trust my clients because I trust myself, which helps them to trust me. It starts with me making that choice – to trust or not. It is a choice, but it's a vulnerable choice.

I'm transparent about the fact that my leadership is also under the spotlight. It's not a given that the horses will move for me. My leadership has to be compelling too. When clients hear this, they are surprised but they realize we are in it together. I'm walking alongside them, willing to be equally vulnerable and to learn in the process.

This sets the tone for the day. When I role model trust and vulnerability with ease, it gives permission for my clients to do the same. They establish trust with the horses in seconds in their first interaction with them, despite being scared. The horses will not go with people if they do not have trust as a basis for the relationship. The moment a client stops trusting the horse, the horse stops and refuses to move. The horse will wait until trust is re-established; as soon as it is, the horse willingly re-engages.

Tiffin and the client feel vulnerable on first meeting

Trust is the foundation for all relationships and is even more critical at times of disruptive change. Although trust is created initially through choice, it is enhanced through listening, dialogue, and connection.

> *A paradigm shift is needed to foster trust in self and others, to let go of the old and allow the new to emerge. The moment we seek control, we cease to trust. Disruptive change requires deeper levels of trust.*

How can you support your team to foster trust in uncertainty?

Vulnerability

We look for certainty to maintain our security. When there is uncertainty, there is vulnerability. Trust requires a level of intimacy that is vulnerable for people who are used to operating behind a mask. Intimacy requires openness, transparency, and honesty so relationships can be built. When you trust yourself enough to be vulnerable, you can drop the mask and create trust with others. Working remotely has increased our vulnerability. You can choose to embrace that vulnerability and let people in, or you can choose to hold them at a distance.

People navigate change in different ways. Disruptive change creates uncertainty and requires flexibility and adaptability out of the comfort zone. Many leaders are comfortable within the known environment but feel less grounded and less confident when operating in the unknown. That's often because they don't have self-awareness and confidence in their leadership capabilities. Leadership happens out of the comfort zone in those moments when you don't know what to think, say or do.

The fear of vulnerability creates a desire to hang on to what is known, often leading to resistance. Alternatively, it causes us to drive something to conclusion quickly so that the answer is understood. When we went into the first COVID-19 pandemic, there was a desire to get on with it and for it to be over quickly. Over time, we've discovered that disruptive change continues to have an impact, far longer than we might initially expect, and the emotional impact goes beyond the practical and logistical change.

Where are you resisting letting go of control and embracing vulnerability?

With so much fear, people become disconnected from their true feelings as a coping mechanism for dealing with stress. Shutting down emotions under stress enables people to function in an almost robotic and disconnected way. With the disconnection from emotions comes a disconnection from others. A fear of vulnerability often causes us to disconnect to protect ourselves and reduce the vulnerability.

Often this disconnection breaks trust; however, we can still trust through disconnection. When you disconnect, trust that it is momentary while you regain your strength to re-engage. When others disconnect, trust that it is not a personal affront towards you; rather, it is their version of self-protection while they work out how to come back. If you trust that people will work things through in their own way, you maintain open channels of communication that speed up the process of them re-engaging and reconnecting.

We can still trust when we hold polarized views – it does not mean that the relationship is broken. When you show others that you trust them in such moments, you create safety for them to return to. Trust is not a one-off activity. It requires a continuous focus to keep rebuilding and deepening relationships.

Where are you disconnecting and what is the impact?

Mistrust

If trust is a choice to step into our vulnerability, we can just as easily create a lack of trust by refusing to be open and vulnerable. A lack of trust is linked to fear – the fear of being hurt, getting things wrong, not being believed or not being good enough. Fear is rife during times of uncertainty and indicates a lack of trust in your own leadership capabilities. If you fail to trust yourself, your approach will be more tentative. When you trust yourself in uncertainty, you create your security by increasing your flexibility and being willing to respond to whatever shows up.

Fear in uncertainty is a lack of trust in our ability to lead or the desire for perfection. We build barriers and hide behind masks of how we want others to see us, as a form of protection. In doing so, we create disconnection that further erodes trust.

Clients often tell me that they don't trust someone because the other person does not trust them. They've reached a stalemate. Each one is waiting for the other to trust first. Someone has to break the downward spiral of mistrust. If you hold the belief that people are inherently good, trust that everyone is doing their best. The media only share negative stories that cause people to lack trust and question others. In parallel, people are doing great work, building communities and enhancing the lives of others. It is a choice: to believe people are inherently good and trust them, or to believe the opposite.

Case study: Robert*

Robert took a long time to trust people, build relationships and let his guard down.

I asked, 'Do you trust me?'

'Yes,' he replied. He had been onsite for about 30 minutes.

He chose to lead Tiffin, a horse who also finds it difficult to trust. Robert took the lead rope and invited Tiffin to go with him. Tiffin followed instantly, completely relaxed. When Robert returned, I asked him whether he trusted Tiffin, and he said he did. He looked surprised. He had just busted his old story that trust takes months to build. Robert's willingness to be vulnerable allowed him to build instant trust. He realized that believing trust took months to build was an old story that shaped the way he approached people at the beginning. Once Robert had reframed his story to say that trust can be built in an instant, he began to drop the masks more and more. He trusted that he could be more honest and transparent with people he didn't know, and he created trust more quickly.

* Name changed to protect confidentiality

Often trust is broken when someone does not behave as you would expect them to. Many people do not seek to rebuild trust once it is broken, and that has a catastrophic effect on teams and organizations. We can choose to trust people even when we don't like their behaviour. By being curious and seeking to understand, trust can be regained, but it requires skill and courage to do this.

Where is trust broken and how can you rebuild it?

Why do we fail to rebuild trust when it is broken? We do it due to fear and self-protection. By holding back on trust, we try to create a barrier of protection, when in fact we make ourselves less safe and secure because the relationship is broken. It is the responsibility of every leader to create trust through open dialogue, connection, and clarity, especially at times of disruptive change and resistance.

Trust is often broken when another person steps over your values, boundaries or beliefs. Often this is done unknowingly, or at least because the other person's values, beliefs and boundaries are different from yours. You can choose to allow trust to remain broken in these moments, or you can engage in open dialogue and be clear about your needs and how this impacts you. When we fail to communicate our needs, we cause further mistrust and miscommunication. Opening the lines of communication without blame and judgement can transform relationships and rebuild trust.

A lack of alignment around common goals can create an unsafe environment, which erodes trust. If we don't have a voice or feel trusted, the environment within which we work feels very unsafe. This increases fear and overwhelm. Trust and transparency are therefore crucial as a foundation for leading through uncertainty and disruptive change.

Mastering uncertainty

- Choose trust as a starting point for every interaction.

- Use vulnerability as a strength to create trust and build relationships.

- Build trust with an open heart, an open mind, honesty, and transparency.

- Be aware of when you hold back or put up a barrier as a result of a lack of trust.

- Notice how fear causes mistrust, and allow yourself to be vulnerable.

- Choose to trust people even when you don't like their behaviour.

- Notice what happens to trust when others disconnect.

- Be curious about the values, boundaries, and beliefs of others when trust is broken and explore the differences openly.

Before you move on to the next chapter, spend 10 minutes reflecting on the levels of trust in yourself, your team and your organization. Reflect on how this impacts your behaviour and interactions with others.

 Download the *Leading Through Uncertainty* workbook from www.judejennison.com/uncertainty and record your reflections.

Provoking personal insight

Which qualities are inherent in your leadership?

Where are you not trusting yourself?

Who else are you not trusting?

Who in your team is struggling to trust in uncertainty?

How can you support your team to foster trust in uncertainty?

Where are you resisting letting go of control and embracing vulnerability?

Where are you disconnecting and what is the impact?

Where is trust broken and how can you rebuild it?

PART 5
WHO'S GOT YOUR BACK?

PART 5

WHO'S GOT YOUR
BACK

Chapter 13

SELF-CARE

'Breathe into possibilities. The answers come when you are grounded, present and have compassion for yourself.'

'What's happening?' I asked the client.

'The horse won't move.'

'How do you feel?'

'Frustrated,' replied the client reluctantly, not wanting to admit to it.

Kalle stood still with her eyes shut. She was unwilling to engage with a frustrated leader.

I asked the client to put their hand where they could feel their breath. They put their hand on their chest.

'Where is your energy in your body?' I asked the client, an unusual question that takes many clients by surprise. They've never considered where their energy is before. The client pointed to their head. They explained that their head was agonizing over how to get Kalle to move. (Some clients point to their chest as they feel the frustration and tension building in their chest, tied in with shallow breathing from the same place.)

Stay grounded

We all experience frustration, at work and in our personal lives. People will engage with us when we are frustrated if they feel they have to, but it damages the relationship in the long term if frustration is the dominant emotion. People are more compliant and collude with hidden emotions, pretending they don't have an impact. By contrast, my horses are less polite. They won't engage with a frustrated leader. Instead, they stand still and refuse to move, often closing their eyes.

Emotions such as frustration and anxiety often lead to being ungrounded, especially in uncertainty. The lack of certainty in disruptive change can cause us to question what to do, how to do it, and how to bring people with us. The dissonance from stress, overwhelm, fear and polarization can cause us to become ungrounded. By paying attention to your embodied leadership, you can identify your underlying emotions, notice any shallow breathing and recover to a more grounded state.

If I ask clients to get grounded, most of them don't know how to do it, or even what it means. When I talk about being grounded, I mean your feet are fully on the floor, your legs feel solid, your breathing is slow and from the diaphragm, and your head is clear and you can think straight. It's you at your most confident and solid. With our fast-paced lives and the volume of uncertainty and change, it's no wonder that we lose our sense of embodied, grounded leadership.

Here's how I re-ground myself:

1. *Breathing.* Notice where you are breathing from and the pace of breathing. Ideally, we should aim for 10 breaths a minute. Breathe in normally for a count of three, feeling the whole of your chest expand from the diaphragm naturally without force. Breathe out for three seconds. You are not trying to do yoga breaths but normal everyday breaths that you can continue (albeit more slowly than when you are ungrounded).

2. *Feet.* Notice how your feet feel on the ground. Are they solidly planted? I imagine myself breathing from the ground up into my feet, all the way to the top of my body, and then breathing out back

down again through the soles of my feet. This shifts the energy from the top of my body to being more balanced throughout the body. You should start to feel your feet more solidly on the ground after a few breaths, and your legs will feel stronger.

3. *Tension.* Notice where there is physical tension in the body – for example, we often raise our shoulders when we are stressed. I often hold tension in my legs. Clients have told me they hold tension in their arms or stomach. Notice what your pattern is and you will get quicker at identifying and releasing it. Simply noticing the tension, you will probably have already reduced it after the breathing. Imagine breathing into any remaining tension and let the tension flow out with your breath through the soles of your feet. Rotate your shoulders, jiggle your legs or move your body about to reduce the tension further.

4. *Head.* Notice whether your head feels clearer at this point and whether you feel calmer. Breathe into any remaining tension and let go of emotions such as frustration or anxiety. Notice if you are hanging onto thoughts about what has just happened or what is about to happen.

5. *Past to future to present.* I imagine my left foot is the past and the right foot is the future. I lean my weight from the past to the future several times back and forth, and then come back to the centre. Notice the present moment when you come back to centre, and keep breathing.

You should feel calmer, more centred, and more present after doing this releasing. I call this 'returning to centre'. This is your embodied leadership from a grounded, centred state and is the place to return to whenever you feel stressed, ungrounded or knocked off balance in some way throughout the day, as we all do. You can do the first four steps while sitting down in a meeting or on a video call, without anyone realizing it. It's a great way to come back to the present whenever you find your emotions taking over.

Be present

Anxiety and frustration occur when we are attached to the past or the future. When we focus on past experiences or become attached to our view of the future, we are no longer present. It is challenging to stay grounded in fast-paced change. It is important not to get caught up in the swell of chaos and become a part of it. Instead, grounded leaders stay present and find ways to alleviate the discomfort without becoming a headless chicken. Many people who have recognized the need for calm have learned to project it externally while feeling something vastly different internally. In order to be congruent and to prevent burnout, we need to find ways to create calm within, not just externally – similar to how I described above. Find your own way to recover when knocked off balance.

We create action in the present moment, and we are more effective when that action comes from a place of grounded leadership rather than from a chaotic response to a crisis. When put under pressure, your adrenaline naturally fires up. That's fine for a short period of time, but it can become exhausting for both you and your team if you continually operate from a place of stress. Continually re-grounding yourself will enable you to be more present and calm, and think more clearly.

> *Learning to be comfortable with not knowing and uncertainty enables us to stay grounded and not invoke the fight/ flight/freeze stress response. This is pivotal to the future of leadership, to minimize stress and overwhelm in uncertainty.*

How grounded are you?

In our fast-paced world, being present is a challenge for many people who live and work at break-neck speed. Spending time with the horses enables people to connect to the natural environment, a well-documented place of rejuvenation and reconnection to self. Horses invite us to a place of stillness from which creativity can occur. Research shows that in the presence of horses, we align our head, heart, and gut. We slow down our breathing and heart rate, become more present and experience a clarity that naturally comes from this calm, grounded place. Many leaders have gained clarity over their most pressing problems by finding this inner state of calm in the midst of great uncertainty. They may not find all the answers, but the next step becomes clear and the grounded sense of calm gives them confidence to move forward into the unknown.

Grounded leaders look after themselves, find moments to disconnect from technology and other people, and find space to recharge. Slowing down enables greater acceptance of the uncertainty and a recognition that it may not be fixable but instead is something to be navigated. If you repeatedly find yourself worrying about the past or the future, find ways to be more present so you can think clearly and create clarity on the next steps.

Breakthroughs always follow uncertainty and chaos. The challenge is to stay grounded in the discomfort long enough to create the transformation.

Let go of control

When teams walk through my gate, their bodies are often tense and conversation is either loud, anxious and boisterous, or subdued, reflective and restrained. Both approaches are signs of the stress of being out of the comfort zone. There is regularly a desire to 'get it right' and save face. It is often matched with exhaustion from overwork. They are ungrounded and not fully present.

Uncertainty is uncomfortable. People desire to hang on to what is known. It's uncomfortable standing in a field about to get honest feedback on your leadership skills... from a horse! Some are sceptical and dismissive, greeting me with 'I don't see the point of this'. Others are quiet and reflective, anxious that they may be 'found out' as not being a good leader. Some are excited about a new experience. Others want to get going quickly before the anxiety takes over.

These are all natural states of responding to not knowing. Each person shows up with their default approach to uncertainty without realizing it. Their default habits and behaviours are unconscious until they work with the horses. Everyone has to let go of who they want to be seen as and step into their authentic leadership.

What is your default approach to uncertainty?

Most education systems are founded on a right or wrong approach. You are rewarded for getting the right answer and reprimanded for doing the wrong thing. This black/white, right/wrong approach is useful for developing a moral compass and cognitive processing like basic maths, but the skills we require to lead disruptive change demand a different style of leadership. A right or wrong approach comes with blame, judgement, and criticism. They are not part of leadership! It assumes that there is only one way of doing things. We struggle to define what leadership is because it is something that we largely feel. You know when you are in flow, and you know when you are not. If you become ungrounded or out of flow, take a breath, let go of judging yourself, and instead re-ground and come back to centre.

Leading through uncertainty requires huge flexibility and adaptability. There can be no right or wrong in uncertainty because the path is unknown, and therefore any approach is untried and untested. When you let go, you allow room for failure and error, and you develop the skills of flexibility, adaptability and agility.

Mr Blue creates a distraction

When we let go of needing to be right, we foster an environment that encourages people to take the next step not knowing where it will take them. New possibilities and opportunities can emerge when we act with curiosity.

Tension comes from attachment, a desire to make things black and white, and for our opinion to be right. It is human to want to do a good job, and we want to encourage great work, but we can do it without creating the stress. With stretch targets and high workloads, it is unrealistic to be able to achieve everything on our to-do list. We need to relinquish control and find a new way of being in relationship with our workloads.

What outcome are you attached to and where is that causing tension?

It is important to let go. When you let go of control, you trust in your leadership. When you trust that whatever happens, you can deal with it, you can let go further and lead disruptive change more confidently. By letting go of control, you step into the discomfort of not knowing and difference.

Letting go does not mean that you absolve yourself of all responsibility. You still hold the desire and the intention, without the attachment to the minute details. When you relinquish the stress and tension of attachment, your leadership flows more easily.

Compassion

Everyone who chooses to lead will experience the glory of success and results, as well as the crushing defeat of failure. We are human after all. Yet with the highs come the lows. To avoid the lows denies us the full human experience. Organizations with a culture of fear of failure inhibit innovation and creativity, and increase stress and pressure.

We sometimes forget to be human. In the pursuit of doing great work, achieving goals, and meeting deadlines and targets, we exert pressure on ourselves and others to avoid failure at all cost. While pressure can enhance our performance for a short period of time, it is not sustainable over longer periods. The cost of excessive pressure is poor physical, emotional, and mental health.

We need more compassion in business – compassion for those who are struggling as well as compassion for ourselves.

We need to shift from trying to be machines in a world of technology to using technology to allow ourselves to be human. When we accept our humanity, we can be kinder to ourselves and to others.

Clients connect when they slow down

We live and work in a time of significant pressure. The volume of workload is immense, and the pressures outside of work continue to grow in parallel. The expectations we place upon ourselves for what we can achieve are often unrealistic. We blame others for that pressure – it's your boss's fault, the shareholders' expectations or the person in your team who is slowing you down by not doing what you want them to do. There is a tension between what is humanly possible and what we think we can achieve in the timescales available.

In this fast-paced techno world, we sometimes attempt to be superhuman. We forget to be kind, compassionate, and considerate towards ourselves. We focus on the results we want to achieve and sometimes on the relationships we want to create or maintain with others. In the process, self-care is overlooked and expectations are unrealistic.

Where do you fit in your daily life?

Often people want to be given permission to be compassionate. They consider it a weakness until they realize how essential it is for themselves as well as for their team. Throughout the COVID-19 pandemic, there was an increased recognition of the need to have compassion for each other. Most leaders made time to check in with members of their team, sometimes on a daily basis. These regular check-ins were not to micro-manage tasks, but to ensure the physical, mental, and emotional wellbeing of their team. Many leaders with whom I worked throughout the pandemic did a fantastic job of looking after their teams, but they did not extend the same compassion to themselves.

As the pandemic continued and employees returned to the office, or at least a hybrid way of working, some leaders continued to hold the same compassion for their team, where others, who perhaps found it a stretch, have long forgotten the need for compassion. Considerate leaders include and embrace everything. They hold compassion for people experiencing challenges. That includes having compassion for yourself as well.

> *How senior leaders behave sets the tone for the organization. Having compassion for yourself and others shows that there is space for humanity, knowing that you will never have 100% full capacity from every single person on every single day.*

Having compassion means acting with self-care to minimize stress and overwhelm. It may mean saying no to unrealistic targets and deadlines, or taking time out to recover and recharge after an especially busy or stressful period at work. Or it may simply be reminding yourself to continually re-ground and return to centre throughout the day. I always say to clients that when it gets difficult, there is another way of doing things. Continually look for ways to reduce stress and tension, and find your flow. Take time out to recharge when needed.

In an interview in January 2018, Sue Grindrod, CEO of the Albert Dock in Liverpool, explained: 'I make sure that I take time out for me. It's important to be kind to yourself, especially when you are under pressure, and to be realistic about what you can actually achieve. If you try to cram everything in, you set yourself up for overwhelm.'[13]

How do you hold yourself with compassion when you are struggling too?

---

[13] Leaders by Nature podcast, 2018, www.leadershipacademy.online/podcasts/leading-through-uncertainty/episodes/2147545523

Who in your team is suffering and needs your compassion?

Case study: Nigel*

'Move over there,' demanded Nigel, pointing to a place on the ground. Kalle stood still, eyes half closed, not moving. As Nigel grew increasingly exasperated by a horse who appeared unwilling and uncooperative, he turned to me and said vehemently, 'This horse is stubborn and won't do it.'

I calmly asked Nigel what he did with people in his team who did not do what he asked them to do. He said he got rid of them. His desire for results was so great that he had no empathy for anyone in his team, even though at his core he was a kind person.

I explained that Kalle wanted kindness, and he was astonished. He had never considered that there might be a different way, and he had no idea how to find it. He had a high turnover in his organization and could not understand why. As soon as it was pointed out to him, Nigel realized that he had been letting good people leave his business, and he wanted to change that. Throughout the day, Nigel learned to soften his approach and give the horse an opinion. As he did so, he found the horse more engaged and more willing to work with him. Some months later, Nigel reported that he was taking time to connect with everyone in his organization and that relationships and teamwork had improved.

* Name changed to protect confidentiality

Compassion for self and others is imperative in challenging times, yet we often overlook it. Continuing to drive ourselves as machines leads to burnout. It's the responsibility of every leader to look out for their team and consider their needs.

> *My wish for the world is that every human being meets every other sentient being with love, compassion, respect, and trust – something we often forget when we are under pressure to achieve results.*

It's time to revert to the core of our humanity, to remember that we are human beings having a human experience. Disruptive change often demands a superhuman approach. We are not machines, and it's up to each and every leader to understand what is humanly possible and to recognize that the benchmark of that is different for everyone. By mastering ourselves, we can raise the energetic vibration of kindness and compassion for ourselves, our families, teams, communities, and the planet. We all deserve and need it.

Mastering uncertainty

- Notice what happens when you become ungrounded.

- Re-ground yourself by taking a breath and feel your feet on the floor.

- Be aware of where you focus on the past and present.

- Return to centre and take action from the present moment.

- Let go of attachment to specific outcomes, and lead with clear intentions.

- Have compassion for yourself as well as others.

- Find ways to reduce your stress and tension.

Before you move on to the next chapter, spend 10 minutes reflecting on your own self-care and compassion. Reflect on how this impacts your behaviour and interactions with others.

 Download the *Leading Through Uncertainty* workbook from www.judejennison.com/uncertainty and record your reflections.

Provoking personal insight

How grounded are you?

What is your default approach to uncertainty?

What outcome are you attached to and where does that cause tension?

Where do you fit in your daily life?

How do you extend compassion to yourself when you are struggling too?

Who in your team is suffering and needs your compassion?

Chapter 14

BUILD YOUR SUPPORT NETWORK

*'People want to help you,
but they don't always know how.'*

Lying face down in a muddy pool of 6 inch-deep water, my head was spinning and pounding. I could hear the sound of someone hammering in the distance.

'Can you hear that banging?' I asked my husband, Paul, who stood beside me. 'Is someone building a house?'

'No, I can't hear anything,' he replied.

'I think I'm concussed,' I said.

'Don't be silly,' Paul replied, as he held out his hand and helped me get to my feet.

I had asked Paul for help as I was struggling to get Kalle in and out of the field. The livery yard where she was kept had moved her to a new field where the gateway was made of electric fence tape and the ground was waterlogged and deep in muddy water. The only way in and out of the field was to open the live electric gate in one hand, lead Kalle through with the other hand, then turn round and hook the gate closed again. When the electric tape touched the wet ground, it sparked with a loud crack, causing Kalle to jump back in fear.

When you know what you are doing, it's a relatively simple manoeuvre to execute, but I was new to this. Everything was uncertain. I had to navigate a pool of muddy water 2 metres wide by 2 metres long, leading a horse with one hand and holding sparking electric tape in the other. The potential risk to our safety was high. In fact, Kalle had already electrocuted us both only a couple of weeks earlier by touching the electric fence while I was leading her. She had reared up and left me shaking in fear. I was doing my utmost not to repeat the experience.

Kalle had repeatedly refused to walk through the gate in the last two days, and I had been unable to get her out of the field. I had a workshop with clients the next day, and I had no idea whether I could get her out to work. I had asked the yard owner if we could switch off the electrics temporarily to help me, and she had refused, saying the other horses might escape. Unsure of where else to turn, I asked my husband to come and hold the gate open so I could focus on leading Kalle through the muddy water. I thought that without the distraction of holding a sparking electric fence gate in the other hand, I might have a bit more success.

It had not gone according to plan. My lack of horsemanship skills was evident, and my leadership skills were lacking, too. I had tried to persuade Kalle to walk through the water, but she was very reluctant. Finally, after much persuasion, she agreed to follow me and started to walk through. I thought we had cracked it. At that moment, I slipped in the mud, and I felt myself falling face down into a pool of brown, murky water. In my unskilled way of leading a horse, I held onto Kalle's lead rope, trying to regain my balance. In doing so, I nearly brought 600 kilograms of horse down on top of me.

Kalle headbutted me out of the way, causing me to drop the lead rope, then she jumped over me to avoid crushing me. I knew in that moment she had done it to save me from serious injury. By contrast, the yard manager told me moments later that Kalle was naughty, badly behaved and had no manners, and that I should have slapped her for headbutting me. She'd been watching at a distance with no offer of support.

I had to admit defeat. I could not look after a horse without adequate support. I am not superhuman. I am not a machine that can be programmed to do things in a particular way, and neither is my horse. I was unskilled and leading through uncertainty with no support. I needed help. Fast. My life and my work depended on it.

Asking for help

Uncertainty and not knowing create stress. They are part of the process of change, innovation and creativity. As the levels of uncertainty in business and throughout the world are amplified, and as innovation and disruptive change generate more uncertainty, so too the level of stress in the workplace increases. There is no quick fix for this, and it is not going to disappear. We cannot expect to navigate our current life and working environments without stress. Instead, we need to learn to find ways to support ourselves and each other to navigate challenges without reaching burnout and overwhelm.

I've spent my life doing what seems ordinary to me and extraordinary to others. I work at a fast pace, achieve high volumes of output in a short space of time and do things that everyone tells me are not possible. I like a challenge. I'm determined and motivated. I persevere when others give up. But I too have my limits. In the moment when I was face down in mud with mild concussion, I had to admit I had reached them.

With little horse knowledge, a 600 kilogram powerful and opinionated horse and a yard where all I received was criticism, I knew I needed the right kind of support instead of constant blame and judgement for not doing things their way. I had repeatedly been open to listening to their advice and working together, but I drew the line at slapping my horse. My way was clearly different. It was time to move on and try a new approach with people who could help me in the way I needed.

Where are you struggling, and who do you need to ask for help?

People often avoid asking for help out of fear of being seen as weak and unable to cope. In fact, asking for help is a sign of strength.

Asking for help shows that you accept the boundaries of your capabilities and recognize that a team can be stronger when supporting each other.

How can you create a culture where people feel safe to ask for help?

When my clients work with my horses, if someone is unable to move a horse, the rest of the team often feels uncomfortable watching. It is common for the team observing to want to offer support, but team members often hold back for fear of not knowing whether an offer of help would be accepted, not knowing how to help and not wanting to diminish or insult the person they can see struggling. Nobody wants to watch others struggle. The person leading often doesn't consider asking for help because they would label it as a failure.

'Not knowing' is a concept so many leaders struggle with. They desire certainty and answers, yet there is little certainty and no perfect answer in an economic environment requiring disruption, innovation and collaboration. People fear asking for help as much as they struggle to offer it, because offering and asking for help create further uncertainty in relationship. Uncertainty requires vulnerability, a willingness to work things through together, a leap of faith into the unknown in partnership. Most people find it easier to struggle on their own than to step into the vulnerability of relying on others for help.

Following a discussion on this, teams learn to offer support instead of diving in and taking over. They learn to be willing to have the offer rejected without taking it personally. They also learn to ask for help from others in return, being clear about what kind of help they want. By being open and transparent in the conversation around support and help, teams discover how to be in relationship in uncertainty without needing to have all the answers. They work together better, speed up success, and minimize failure and discomfort for everyone. Asking for help can be transformative for both individuals and teams. There is no need to struggle alone.

Network and community

Our communities look very different today from how they did in the 20th century. Local communities have become global. We rely on technology to connect us, but human connection is what really creates community. Build your own communities of different people so that you are supported in times of uncertainty, according to what you need in any given moment. These communities can be virtual and/or local. Find a combination that supports your need for support and connection.

Throughout the COVID-19 pandemic, many entrepreneurs turned to each other for support. Disruptive change sometimes requires different perspectives to shed light on a situation. Have the humility to not have all the answers, and look to collaboration to solve key problems. I'm part of a number of entrepreneurial networks, as well as professional bodies, and many of us reached out to each other, sometimes to share ideas, sometimes to ask for feedback, sometimes for emotional support.

I also have a couple of friends who run their own businesses, and we regularly call each other up if we need a friendly ear or someone to kick us into touch. Knowing that someone has your back through disruptive change is critical to staying grounded and also sense-checking your direction. Disruptive change will always create uncertainty which will continue to cause us to doubt ourselves, or worse, act without thinking things through carefully. Building a support network is essential to prevent your family from taking the brunt of rising frustration or work stresses and strains.

Most people have no idea that their colleagues support them. They never ask for help because they believe it will lead to them being disrespected. Instead they struggle on, not knowing how to do something, feeling more and more under pressure to perform and to create results when nothing is certain.

Who needs your support?

Who might support you if you asked?

> *There is a need to move from blame, judgement, and criticism to a culture of support. More collaborative ways of working can ensure everyone gets support from each other to navigate their challenges.*

Formal mentoring programmes can be enormously helpful, and informal ones can be just as useful. I have numerous informal mentors who I talk to when I get stuck. I rarely need to push through on my own. Just being listened to and sharing your challenge is helpful because you gain clarity by giving voice to the issue. It moves from a jumble in your head to a clear problem that can be worked on, with support from others who are less emotionally charged around the issue.

Uncertainty is challenging and uncomfortable, and there are no prizes for being a hero and going it alone. The most common thing I hear CEOs, MDs and executives say is how lonely they are at the top. They feel unsupported, yet they need only to ask for help or advice and people will provide support. Throughout the pandemic, this feeling of responsibility and being alone increased for many people. I encouraged clients to turn to their teams and find the solutions together. It helped teams to feel included and recognize that everyone was vulnerable. It takes courage for leaders to do this with their teams, and there is a time and a place when it is appropriate to do it.

Giving voice to a problem can remove the emotional charge from it, as long as it is done in a positive way. When you express righteous indignation, you release dopamine into your system, which gives you an initial good feeling. This is an addictive hormone, which means you are likely to repeat the same frustration over and over. Organizations can quickly build up a culture where people complain with no intention of taking responsibility for doing anything about it. This leads to constant negativity. Notice where you are expressing righteous indignation. You have a choice over how you want to respond. You can either ignore the situation (in which case, drop the moaning) or decide what action you want to take, finding support as you do so. Focus on what you want and need, rather than what you don't want.

Most people believe that they are being criticized by others. When you reach out to others for support, they are usually willing to help. If people are stretched, they may not be able to help every time, but it does not mean they don't care. Everyone is under pressure. Give people a chance to provide support and be mutually supported. Recognize also when they cannot, and do not take it personally.

We need to shift from a culture of disconnection and discomfort to one of connection, relationship and community. This requires a willingness to be truly seen and to trust that whatever happens in uncertainty, we can navigate it together. After all, our ability to come together when needed is the core of our humanity. If we can come together in moments of crisis, we can connect on an everyday basis too. Business will be all the better for it and so will the human race.

Virtual communities

Many of us were already part of virtual communities prior to the COVID-19 pandemic. Technology enables us to come together from all over the world based on shared interests and passions. I've met people online through my work as an Equine Facilitated Leadership practitioner and developed relationships with other practitioners from all over the world. It allows us to collaborate with each other, learn together, and provide peer mentoring support. When we eventually meet at physical conferences, we instantly recognize each other, and we feel as though we already know each other. When you have met people online first, it makes it easier to go to large conferences as there are familiar faces which reduce the feeling of being isolated and alone in a crowd.

There is no substitute for being together face to face. Often there is the surprise of seeing someone in 3D and realizing that they are taller or shorter than expected, and the relationship deepens as you have the full embodied sense of that person.

As we combine working in the office with remote working, we must pay attention to how this impacts performance and engagement. Over time, the emotional connection to the organization can reduce if people don't feel connected. You can build virtual communities over shared passions or key pieces of work; however, it cannot match the connection that is created locally and face to face.

A Gallup article summarizing the report *Women in America: Work and Life Well Lived* identified that 'women who strongly agree they have a best friend at work are more than twice as likely to be engaged (63%) compared with the women who say otherwise (29%)'.[14] The research doesn't stop there. There is value to having engaged employees. The article continues: 'When employees possess a deep sense of affiliation with their team members, they are driven to take positive actions that

---

[14] Gallup, 'Women in America: Work and life well-lived', 2018, www.gallup.com/workplace/238070/women-america-work-life-lived-insights-businessleaders.aspx

benefit the business – actions they may not otherwise even consider if they did not have strong relationships with their co-workers.'

How do you create emotional connection with a community in a virtual environment?

Don't go it alone

Scientific studies on social isolation have tended to focus on how it impacts cognitive decline in people over the age of 60. It may be some years before we understand the impact on our mental health of social isolation from the COVID-19 pandemic. The leading mental health organization in the United Kingdom, Mind, outlines a number of problems caused by loneliness, including 'increased risk of depression, anxiety, low self-esteem, sleep problems, and increased stress'.[15] Most of us have noticed the impact of the pandemic on our mental health and have sought different ways to counteract it.

We all remember those early days of the COVID-19 pandemic lockdowns where everyone found different coping mechanisms – some turned to video calls with family, friends, and colleagues, sharing meals via Zoom. Others turned to fresh air and exercise, while yet others took up new hobbies and found virtual communities with which to share their passion. We often find coping mechanisms in the short term, but many of them are not sustainable. Those heady days of wearing a hat on Zoom to entertain your colleagues are long gone, but the remote working remains.

How do you stay connected now in a hybrid way of working?

Many people wanted to help others and responded to pandemic lockdowns with offers of support in the local community. As hybrid working becomes the norm, and we learn to work from home and the office, we must find proactive ways to stay connected to colleagues, to be supported as well as offering support. Our physical and mental health as well as our business results will depend on it.

---

[15] Mind, 'Loneliness', 2021, www.mind.org.uk/information-support/tips-for-everyday-living/loneliness/about-loneliness

Mastering uncertainty

- Ask for help. People want to provide support.

- Asking for help is vulnerable and a strength.

- Offer support to others, and be willing to have the offer rejected without taking it as a personal affront.

- Create an environment of openness and transparency so your team feels comfortable asking for help.

- There is little certainty in disruptive change so working together is crucial.

- Use technology to create virtual communities of support and collaboration.

- Giving voice to problems can reduce the emotional charge to them.

- Social isolation impacts mental health. Don't go it alone.

Before you move on to the next chapter, spend 10 minutes reflecting on who needs your support and who can support you.

 Download the *Leading Through Uncertainty* workbook from www.judejennison.com/uncertainty and record your reflections.

Provoking personal insight

Where are you struggling, and who do you need to ask for help?

How can you create a culture where people feel safe to ask for help?

Who needs your support?

Who might support you if you asked?

How do you create emotional connection with a community in a virtual environment?

How do you stay connected now in a hybrid way of working?

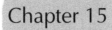

Chapter 15

LEAD FROM THE HEART AND SOUL

'Leading with passion and purpose brings people alive.'

When Kalle arrived in December 2011, I sensibly put her in a full livery yard so that someone else could look after her and I could learn from them. With my lack of horse knowledge, I needed all the support I could get, and I thought this would ease the pressure for me. It didn't. The livery yard handled its horses very differently, using coercion and control. I learned a lot about how I did *not* want to be in relationship with Kalle. To be clear, these were kind people who loved their horses, but in the same way that people in business use force and control to get people to do things, they expected their horses to follow the rules.

I had different ideas and different values. I wanted to lead Kalle in a way that enabled her to keep her majestic spirit and to live and work with free will. I wanted to be in relationship and work together to do extraordinary work. I want the same for people in my team, too. The relationship I wanted to have with Kalle was one of partnership, respect, trust, love, and connection. I refused to resort to force or dominance, but I was unskilled in knowing another way. That's what uncertainty often brings – a need for trial and error. Fail, recover, and begin again.

In the first few days, Kalle ran rings round me, sometimes literally. She was often on her toes, spinning round in front of me, snorting in fear. She spooked at everything. I mirrored her fear, terrified she might trample me or knock me over. I had no idea how to look after a horse, and I was finding my way, working it out as I went along. I ignored the books and the contradictory horsemanship advice and followed my intuition. I drew on every ounce of my corporate leadership experience to understand Kalle's needs and develop a relationship. I knew that every time Kalle took the lead, it was because she didn't have confidence in my leadership, so I had to keep stepping up. I listened and paid attention to her feedback and tried a different approach.

The yard staff became increasingly irritated with me for not following their coercive instructions. They said she was naughty and needed to be slapped. I saw her fear and wanted to help her find her confidence instead. I knew that my leadership and my own confidence in uncertainty would be the breakthrough that we both needed. The control they used with their horses, they also tried to use with their clients like me. While other clients did as they were told and slapped their horses, I refused to. My stress levels began to rise. I so badly wanted to belong but I was clearly very different, not least because I didn't ride. I wanted to learn from their experience, but I knew that when I followed my instincts and really listened to Kalle, we understood what our way was. We were working together, in a relational way.

True relationship, true partnership, true co-creation. I was unskilled in knowing how to create that with a horse in those early days. Every night I went home in tears and told my husband I couldn't do it anymore. He sat and listened without judgement. When I asked whether I should give it up or continue, he always responded that he knew I would find my way and make my own decisions. I'm grateful for that freedom of choice. He never disempowered me by telling me what to do.

I stayed. I stayed when I was face down in mud with concussion. I stayed when Kalle electrocuted us both and reared up, retriggering my trauma around horses. I stayed when we looked each other in the eye in a moment of pure connection as we collapsed on our knees when the farrier beat her for not standing still. I stayed even though I sobbed uncontrollably for two hours afterwards. I stayed through one drama after another (many documented in my previous book, *Leadership Beyond Measure*) because sometimes leading from the heart and soul requires it and because I was leading in service of my clients who were gaining breakthroughs from working with us. Every morning, I got up and tried again. Over the first six months, I was in and out of overwhelm. I had no idea how to look after a horse and no idea how to run a business either, and here I was trying to learn both in parallel.

I became exhausted and overwhelmed by the responsibility. I had gone beyond the realm of uncertainty to unskilled and unsafe. Something had to change. I sought help from Kalle's previous owner and asked her to take Kalle back temporarily. She provided support for the next six weeks while I rebuilt my confidence and found a new place for Kalle to live, a place where we could both relax and find our way together without being told what to do and without needing to use force of any kind. I created a framework of support so I could continue.

I'm still here, leading and learning. I have more skill, my own land and the most incredibly relaxed and happy herd, but the uncertainty continues. On a daily basis, uncertainty rears its head, and I find a way to move forward.

Jude leading four of her herd (left to right, Kalle, Tiffin, Jude, Mr Blue, Gio)

Embodying uncertainty

Uncertainty requires us to step into the unknown. We may think we know where we are going, but we don't always know how to get there. Along the way, things pop up that we cannot foresee and that we cannot fathom. The COVID-19 pandemic for one! Somehow, we recover and carry on, including those new experiences and the associated learning in our path. There is no manual or how-to guide to deal with the unknown. We lead our way through it, sometimes with ease, sometimes with discomfort.

I published the first edition of this book in 2018, long before the COVID-19 pandemic. The content was relevant long before COVID-19 but the pandemic took uncertainty to another level for all of us. When we went into lockdown, my business closed as people could no longer come and work face to face. The costs of looking after a herd of horses continued. I pivoted so many times I was nearly spinning. I've lived and breathed every word in this book. Throughout the pandemic, I repeatedly picked up this book for guidance when I felt the stress and overwhelm of trying to keep a business afloat, the fear and polarization, the trauma of nearly coming close to having my horses put to sleep if I couldn't make my business work. Throughout, I have drawn on my leadership to move one foot in front of the other, knowing that I always have options, even when the path is unclear.

The path of uncertainty is an emotionally challenging one. I hope this book has given you a better understanding of why that is and what that means for you as a leader, as well as how you can support yourself, as well as your team and organization. We cannot pretend that the emotions don't exist.

> *We experience fear and polarization, stress and overwhelm, in varying degrees, when we lead through uncertainty. We are all resilient to a point, and resilience differs for everyone. We cannot continue to put ourselves under inordinate pressure without realizing that it has a long-term impact on individuals, organizations and society.*

This book has been challenging to write because it describes *embodied leadership,* and it invites you to find *your* new way, which is always going to be different from mine. We can't plan ahead and expect every-thing to fall into place and people to do what we want, when we want, how we want. We are not machines. We can't turn emotional responses on and off like a tap. We have to process them, work with them and learn to lessen the grip they have on us, knowing that they will always be a part of leading through uncertainty and disruptive change. That is a work in process – a lifetime of learning and a continuous cycle of increasing self-awareness.

We live in extraordinary times. We need to evolve the human species through conscious leadership, being mindful of the impact we have in each and every moment. The skills needed to influence others and create human connection are not easy to develop. We need to embody them and find ways to develop ourselves in a safe environment, with continuous feedback and space for reflection, based on scientific evidence.

It is a privilege to witness clients experiencing this when working with my herd of horses, who give so freely to enable transformational learning. They invite us to change our world view, to amend our habits and behaviours, to influence the future and create work that is life-en-hancing in a world that we want to leave behind for future generations. That's a big ask from a development experience, yet it's what I offer to my clients.

It's now 10 years since Kalle came into my life. In that time, I have taken on seven horses, helped them to recover from previous ailments (physical and emotional) and rehabilitated one of them to go to a new home as he was not safe to work with clients and had recovered suffi-ciently to be ridden again. I held Opus and Gio as they were put to sleep, and I supported the rest of the herd as they experienced their own sense of loss and worked through their grief. I've experienced highs and lows and learned so much. It takes courage to do what feels right, knowing you don't have all the answers.

I've built a solid team around me, safe in the knowledge and wisdom that I can lead confidently and securely through uncertainty. Except when I don't. I have my limits, too. Yet I do know that in the moments when I falter, I build the resilience to come back stronger.

Uncertainty is uncomfortable. It is an opportunity to learn as a leader, to develop new skills, to find new ways of working and to achieve extraordinary things. It can derail us and cause confusion. Whenever we are not in flow, we have the choice to recover to that state, to dig deeper in our leadership, to find new ways of doing things, to fail, recover, and try again.

How do you continually modify your behaviour to meet an ever-changing, fast-paced environment?

Leading through uncertainty requires a new mindset. Although emotional and social intelligence have increasingly been recognized as essential components of leadership, they have largely been engaged from the intellect. We need to shift from the analysis of emotions to empathic understanding and emotional engagement.

A new way of leading from the heart and soul is called for as we embrace the next evolution of leadership, with courage and compassion in abundance. We need to *feel* our leadership.

Leaders who have a sense of purpose and passion for their work feel alive, and are engaging and inspiring to others. They feel compelled to go above and beyond what is expected of them, recognizing the emotional fallout of uncertainty, finding new ways of leading from the heart and soul.

Jude leading Gio

FINAL THOUGHTS

As I stand in the field after a workshop with clients, the horses graze calmly beside me. There is incredible peace around me and within me. Each one of them has taught me so much and will continue to do so. They give freely and willingly, sometimes being gentle with me when I am vulnerable and afraid, sometimes headbutting me into next week when I am dithering and uncertain. That doesn't happen too often!

Kalle in particular expects me to lead by example. If I don't lead my business and the herd, nobody else will. It's my role, and one I step up to with passion, joy, and enthusiasm – most of the time. Sometimes it feels lonely at the top. I know many CEOs experience that, too. I have plenty of mentors who offer advice and guidance, but ultimately it's my responsibility to lead my business, the herd, and my clients. They all expect it of me.

The horses are soft yet powerful. They know their purpose is intertwined with mine – to lead others to find their inner peace so that we all have the skills to live and work in harmony with others. I watch and learn. I notice when they set boundaries and articulate their needs with clarity. I watch Kalle stand solidly in self-assured presence – blending power and gentleness, clarity and compassion. She has a massive range of leadership skills and is an incredible role model of a female leader who loses none of her femininity while standing strongly with a powerful presence.

People often tell me how happy the horses are. My horses move a lot, play a lot and seem utterly content with their lives. I want to lead a team with a zest for life, joy for their work and a desire to make a difference. The horses certainly do all of that. Every horse who has arrived has come with emotional or physical challenges. Over time, I see them relax into the herd, start to bring more and more of their personality and individuality. They become more challenging to lead once they realize they have full expression of their opinion. I'm willing to be challenged, willing to step up as a leader, knowing that they benefit greatly from having full expression of themselves, as people do too. I try to extend the same leadership qualities to my human team, continually asking myself, 'What do they need from me now?'

Uncertainty requires the flexibility and willingness to keep trying, keep learning, keep making a difference. It matters. Your leadership matters. We live in extraordinary times where everything seems in flux. One of my clients, a CEO of a large corporation, once said, 'I have learned to lead from my spirit, and I can't tell you how powerful that is.' There was a brief moment when her executive team stood spellbound. It was as if the world had stopped, and everyone held their breath. Then it began again, changed forever. This is true leadership, from the heart and soul. This is what I wish for everyone to experience, and this is what I wish for the world. I know we can do great things when we lead from our heart and soul, with courage and compassion, with a desire to leave a legacy that matters in the world. I know that matters to you, to me, and to everyone.

In the heart of the Midlands, in the middle of the English country-
side, there is a field. A place of uncertainty. A place where you step
through the gate into the unknown, unsure whether your leadership
stacks up the way you thought it did. There you discover that despite
the uncertainty, you are safe, you are held, and you are powerful.
The horses and I will meet you there.
Join us. The world needs you.

With love,
Jude

MEET THE EQUINE TEAM

Every business needs a high-performing team, and I'm grateful to have handpicked mine. All of my horses are rescue horses. They have been retired from riding careers for various reasons. None of them can now be ridden, so they come to me to do a new job.

I choose horses who are safe to work with novices because most clients have no experience around horses, and many are anxious on arrival. Every horse that has come to me has a new sense of purpose and when I take them, I commit to providing a home for life. That's a big responsibility, especially when the youngest is only nine.

Each of my horses has started working with clients within days of arrival. They are curious about the work and interested. Often when we work with one or two horses in the arena, the others will stand at the fence line, watching. The newer ones learn by observing the experienced ones, much as a human team would. They all bring different skills and respond in different ways, with vastly different personalities, which often surprises people.

I keep them as a natural herd as much as possible, and they live out in the fields 24/7, all year round. People often comment on how happy the horses seem and how much they play. I think if we provide an environment where people or horses can thrive, they are happy and want to do their best work. That's certainly true of my team.

Here is the Leaders by Nature team.

Kalle

Kalle is a black 16.2 hands Trakehner mare, born in April 2000. Trakehners are a German breed and a mix of Arab and thoroughbred breeding. They are highly sensitive, and often riders describe them as tricky. In fact, I find them to be very straightforward and

extremely suitable for my work. They want to work in partnership, and they don't like to be told what to do. It makes them ideal for this work because they need you to balance absolute clarity and direction with a strong relationship, and to invite them to work *with* you, not *for* you. If you listen to them and pay attention to their needs, they are very willing.

Kalle was my first horse and started this work in January 2012. She is highly intuitive and she knows which buttons to press to give you great learning. She has a massive range and can bring whatever is needed to give clients the best learning. She will headbutt you into next week if she thinks you are not listening to her or not giving her enough respect. By contrast, she will treat you like a foal if you are terrified. She knows when to challenge and when to back off and be gentle. She can switch from one end of her leadership range to the other in an instant.

When she first arrived, she was often on her toes, snorting in fear at everything that was new. Her power was obvious and explicit, yet clients were willing to work with her, wanting to challenge themselves and learn. Now she has a self-assured presence that people often find intimidating. Many clients avoid her at the beginning of the day, thinking she will be challenging. In fact, she is extremely gentle and kind, and as long as you blend clarity, direction and relationship in equal measure, she follows you anywhere willingly. Learning from her is guaranteed.

While Kalle is hugely committed to helping clients learn, she accepts nothing less than my very best leadership. She is the leader of the herd, so when she moves, everyone else follows. She therefore requires a confident, clear leader before she will relinquish her lead. In moments of uncertainty, she demands that I lead from the front, with confidence, clarity and purpose. She'll have nothing to do with me unless I am on top form. She reminds me that even when I am uncertain, I have a choice to be a powerful leader or not.

It is a privilege to work and learn with her.

Opus

Opus came to me in July 2012, aged 24, when he retired from his riding career. He was a 16.1 hands dark brown thoroughbred. He was a descendant of a horse called Northern Dancer, the highest-earning racehorse of all time. Opus was born in Australia in 1988 and lived in New Zealand, Bahrain and then the United Kingdom, so he was well travelled and the most experienced of the herd in terms of riding experiences. He competed in just about everything with his owner, Laura.

Opus was challenging with CEOs, MDs, executive teams and senior leaders because he expected them to lead without dominance. With graduates, he was gentle and easy, so they went away with more confidence. Opus took charge unless you matched his alpha male presence. Whereas Kalle requires a softer energy, Opus required a strong, masculine energy in order for him to pay attention. However, if you raised your energy too much, you could easily enter a power struggle with him. Opus demanded that you find that knife-edge of assertiveness in order for him to come with you.

Opus had the free run of the yard and was the welcoming party to clients, sometimes not letting them through the gate! He would stand outside my office, watching every sales meeting I ever had, and regularly demand hobnobs, his favourite biscuit.

Opus decided who he wanted to work with. He would kick the gate and demand to be let in to work with someone. He would march up to a chosen person, head butt them as if to say 'You, work with me.' It was a privilege for clients to be chosen by him. He missed nothing, and I always knew he had my back.

Opus passed away in August 2019. He continues to have an impact on clients through the stories we tell about him.

Tiffin

Tiffin was the third horse to join me, in June 2014, at the age of 13. He is a dark bay 16.3 hands Irish thoroughbred, born in Ireland in April 2001. He raced in Ireland and was brought to England to hunt. He was sold every year for four consecutive years. The last place he

lived was a riding school where he sometimes did great work and sometimes exploded and bucked everyone off.

Having been sold repeatedly, and his home never being quite right for him, I was Tiffin's last chance at life – a responsibility I take very seriously. When he had his meltdown (described in Chapter 6), I wondered whether he would be better with a more experienced horse owner, but I persevered as I wanted him to find security in his home. I'm glad I did as he has turned a major corner in his work and teaches clients about confidence and trust.

When Tiffin arrived, he looked older than his years. His face was misshapen, and I thought he had possibly taken a tumble during his racing or hunting days to cause this. Over time, as he has relaxed into his home, his face has become gentler, he looks younger, and I realize that his misshapen face was the tension of stress and anxiety.

Tiffin had a difficult start in life and connects deeply with others who have physical or emotional challenges. He will often connect with the person who is emotionally struggling, or he will touch injured parts of the body with his nose. He struggles to work with dominant men, as I believe they remind him of his past. He supports Kalle in leading the herd and keeps the young boys in check. He has become more playful as he relaxes and is often the one to instigate a boxing match with the young boys, inviting them to rise up on their hind legs and play with him.

Tiffin works better on a one-to-one basis as he often finds the energy and anxiety of a team overwhelming. Tiffin is deep and highly sensitive. He has difficulty trusting people, but if you trust him absolutely, he will join you in that place.

Mr Blue

Mr Blue arrived in October 2015, aged only five years. He is a 16.2 hands grey Trakehner gelding. He had arthritis by the age of five, which meant he was severely lame when he came to me. He was still a very young horse who had no idea where his feet were and often stumbled over them and made us laugh. While he will never be ridden, he now moves more smoothly, and his feet, back and knees are much stronger.

Mr Blue loves people and is highly interactive. He is the class clown and likes to goof around. He pushes the boundaries and took the longest to integrate into the herd because he didn't pay attention to herd behaviour. He invades personal space repeatedly, and the other horses have to be very clear with him. He does it gently, out of a desire for a close connection, but needs to be put in his place regularly.

He does the same with people and likes to pick up their feet with his teeth. If you let him, he pushes the boundaries further, and he has been known to steal hats and gloves from clients. Mr Blue provides a lot of the humour and fun on workshop days. He loves toys and is easily distracted, so he causes teams to get derailed on a regular basis unless they are extremely focused and clear and work as a cohesive unit.

Mr Blue reminds us not to take life so seriously and to make leadership fun. He also shows how to balance playfulness without losing respect or focus. Often clients who get easily distracted or love to play have a hard time with him because he takes advantage of them. He derails people by messing about and causing a distraction. Mr Blue teaches clients the balance of when to have fun and when to be focused to get the job done.

Gio

Gio joined the Leaders by Nature team in June 2017 at the age of seven. He was Mr Blue's half-brother, although they looked very different. He was a 17.2 hands black Trakehner gelding who was never ridden due to ongoing lameness. He had the sweetest personality, and this was his first job.

Although Gio was the largest of the herd by far, he was the gentlest, and he connected on a deep level. He liked to nuzzle your ear and breathe into your nose. He was the first to look up when you went into the field and often the first horse to come over. He was interested in all clients and loved the work. He created a heart-to-heart connection and was often the one that clients wanted to take home at the end of the day. He trusted people willingly and readily.

The master of compassion, Gio had a massive heart, and in his presence, you could feel your own heart expanding as you stood with him. Gio passed away suddenly in November 2019, aged nine years. Adored by everyone, Gio was a gentle giant and is missed terribly.

Admiral

 The newest and youngest of my team, Admiral was born in 2012. He joined the team in November 2019 a week after Gio's death. He is Mr Blue's (and Gio's) half-brother, all sharing the same Trakehner father. His mother is a breed called Holsteiner, a large carthorse breed. Admiral is the tallest of the herd, standing at 17.3 hands high. He was injured in the field when he was two years old so has never been ridden. As a result, he has the least life experience of all of my horses and is a bit like a gentle but clumsy foal in a large body.

The first time I went to pick his feet up, he shook me off so hard, I nearly went through the fence. He looked surprised at how physically strong he is and how weak I am in comparison! He has learnt to be gentler with us and is willing and curious about the work with clients. He works well with clients when loose in the field and is often the first horse to come over and meet someone new. He is less sure of himself in the arena in more controlled exercises and can be anxious when led with a head collar, typically because clients are anxious leading him, and he picks up on their insecurity.

Admiral is unsure of himself in uncertainty and requires a lot of clarity, confidence and direction, just as an inexperienced member of a human team would who is new to their job. He is still finding his feet and his confidence is growing.

ACKNOWLEDGEMENTS

The writing of this book was primarily a solitary process, but the overall result is a team effort. I am hugely grateful to everyone who provided input and support along the way, from the conception of the idea to the completed book.

Firstly, thank you Pepsi, my former black Labrador, who sat with me in a field for four days. The output of that time was the title of this book. It was at least a start!

A huge thank you to the contributors to this book – Susan Gee from Yorkshire Water, Elizabeth Cronin from the New York State Office for Victim Services and Colin D Smith, aka The Listener. Their contributions highlight practical examples of the concepts in this book, demonstrating their importance in different working environments.

The CEOs I interviewed for this book gave me their precious time and great insights into their worlds – Nigel Newton, Sue Noyes, Elizabeth Cronin, Sondra Scott, Gina Lodge, Bridget Shine, Peter Istead, Sue Grindrod, Nick Eastwood, Paul Faulkner and many others through more informal conversations.

I continue to interview executives for my podcasts, and their stories were invaluable in shaping the final book. Thank you also to my clients over the years. I have learned from each one, and it was an honour and a privilege to witness the depth of learning and to learn alongside them.

A team of mentors and support buddies helped me from start to finish. My writing buddy Wendy Prior tolerated me for a week's writing retreat, during which I prevaricated and procrastinated while she got on with writing. She kicked me into action and got me off to a great start, despite my resistance. My book mastermind buddies Michael Brown, Elaine Halligan, and Anne Archer challenged and supported me in equal measure throughout the writing process. Tom Evans provided guided meditations to help me find my flow whenever I got stuck, which was quite often.

Thank you to my publisher, Alison Jones of Practical Inspiration Publishing, who believed in me from the moment we met via Facebook.

In the moments when I think I might abandon the idea of writing this book, Alison's unfailing belief in me keeps me going.

I extend enormous gratitude to John Palmer, who beta read the first draft of the first edition of this book in great detail, highlighting everything he disagreed with, as well as highlighting the parts he thought were great. John's incredibly thoughtful feedback gave me confidence in some of what I'd written and helped me turn the dodgy sections from a series of mutterings into the final book.

Thank you to John Cleary for the photographs in the book and Jerry Longland for the illustrations. You are two people who continually provide support that is way beyond your remit.

To my husband Paul, who never complains as I spend long hours writing while he runs around after me and provides meals and lots of tea.

Finally, I'm blessed to have the most incredible mentors in the form of my equine team – Kalle, Opus, Tiffin, Mr Blue, Gio, and Admiral. They may not have been much use in the writing process, but much of what I've learned about leading through uncertainty is as a result of working with them.

In the end, it was a team effort. I did the writing but the extensive conversations, learning, feedback, and support shaped this book.

Thank you everyone. Here's to the next one!

ABOUT THE AUTHOR

Jude Jennison is an award-winning executive team coach, author and speaker, specializing in leading through uncertainty and disruptive change. A business owner since 2010, Jude previously worked for IBM for 17 years, where she managed a budget of US$1 billion and led UK, European, and global teams.

Jude develops the leadership skills of executive teams and entrepreneurs to accelerate business results through greater clarity, connection, and commitment. She works with a herd of horses to uncover the default patterns of non-verbal communication that enable leaders and teams to be more effective out of their comfort zone. She has coached over 4000 leaders and teams.

Jude is an international speaker on leadership matters and the author of the books *Leadership Beyond Measure, Leading Through Uncertainty*, and *Opus: The Hidden Dynamics of Team Performance*.

Jude has been featured on BBC Two and BBC Radio 4, as well as being featured in the FT, Virgin Entrepreneur, and local radio and press. She is a regular writer for *HR Director* magazine.

Jude is the Founder of Leaders by Nature and the creator of LeadershipAcademy.Online. She was cited #3 in the Thinkers 360 list for Top 100 Global Thought Leaders and Influencers you should follow in 2021.

Contact Jude

 www.judejennison.com

 Jude@judeJennison.com

 judejennison

 jude.jennison

 leadersbynature

 judejennison

INDEX